C000314479

Stephen Cottrell has been Bishop of (Bishop of Reading before that. He Naughty Nora in many schools. Peterborough Cathedral, Stephen has a wealth of experience in building up the faith of the worshipping community and helping to develop mission and ministry. Stephen has worked as a full-time evangelist and teacher about mission with Springboard, the Archbishops' initiative for evangelism, and has written widely about evangelism. He is one of the authors of *Emmaus: The Way of Faith*, a programme for evangelism, nurture and discipleship that is now used by about 3000 churches in Britain and around the world. Among his many books, his work includes *I Thirst: the Archbishop of Canterbury's Lent Book for 2004* (Zondervan, 2003), *From the Abundance of the Heart: Catholic Evangelism for All Christians* (DLT, 2006), *Do Nothing to Change Your Life; Discover What Happens When You Stop* (Church House Publishing, 2007), *The Things He Carried* (SPCK, 2008), *The Things He Said* (SPCK, 2009), *Hit the Ground Kneeling* (Church House Publishing, 2010) and *Come and See: Learning from the life of Peter* (BRF, 2011). Stephen is married to Rebecca and enjoys telling stories to his three sons, Joseph, Benjamin and Samuel.

Text copyright © Stephen Cottrell 2008
The author asserts the moral right
to be identified as the author of this work

Published by
The Bible Reading Fellowship
15 The Chambers, Vineyard
Abingdon OX14 3FE
United Kingdom
Tel: +44 (0)1865 319700
Email: enquiries@brf.org.uk
Website: www.brf.org.uk
BRF is a Registered Charity

ISBN 978 1 84101 388 6
First published 2008
Reprinted 2013
10 9 8 7 6 5 4 3 2 1
All rights reserved

Acknowledgments
Unless otherwise stated, scripture quotations are taken from the Contemporary
English Version of the Bible published by HarperCollins Publishers, copyright
© 1991, 1992, 1995 American Bible Society.

Scripture quotations taken from the Holy Bible, New International Version,
copyright © 1973, 1978, 1984 by International Bible Society, are used by
permission of Hodder & Stoughton Publishers, a division of Hodder Headline
Ltd. All rights reserved. 'NIV' is a registered trademark of International Bible
Society. UK trademark number 1448790.

A catalogue record for this book is available from the British Library

Printed Lightning Source

The Adventures of
Naughty Nora

14 fun stories of everyday life

for collective worship, assemblies and storytelling
in the classroom

Stephen Cottrell

In thanksgiving for the schools and children
with whom I have worked during my ministry

Acknowledgments

Naughty Nora has been to quite a few schools. She started off at Christ Church Church of England Primary School in Forest Hill. She then moved to Parklands County Primary School in Chichester. Most of her schooling was at Lindley Church of England Infants School in Huddersfield and St Thomas More Roman Catholic Primary School in Peterborough. Latterly she has been attending Englefield Church of England Primary School, down the road from where I live. I owe a debt of thanks to all these schools for allowing Naughty Nora in. Her adventures have surprised and delighted a lot of staff and children at these schools.

In particular, I want to thank Sue Drake, former head teacher at Lindley School, who encouraged me to tell these stories and even to start writing them down. I also want to thank my wife, Rebecca, and my three children, Joseph, Benjamin and Samuel. The stories were usually tested on them at home before being told in an assembly. Their comments on the original stories, and then the written versions found here, have been enormously helpful. My niece, Holly, has also read through a couple of the stories for me. Finally, I want to thank Sue Doggett at BRF for encouraging me to turn the stories into a book. My great hope is that this will enable Naughty Nora to travel to many more schools and homes and to delight many more children.

Contents

Foreword

We knew that Naughty Nora was trouble from the first moment Bishop Stephen, or Revd Cottrell as he then was, introduced her to us at Lindley CE (VA) Infant School. Bishop Stephen always had a twinkle in his eye when he told us about her and the children relished listening to every moment of her delicious misdemeanours.

It was fascinating to watch the children as they listened to the stories—especially the faces of those children who could identify closely with Naughty Nora's transgressions. Members of staff frequently appeared in the stories, much to our amusement, and Nora regularly found her way into RE, PSHE and literacy lessons.

Bishop Stephen understands children and knows intuitively how to appeal to their sense of fair play. He knows that they will revel in Nora's wrongdoings but that they will also feel reassured when her parents step in to guide her toward making the right choices, just a loving God guides and supports those who stray.

Bishop Stephen sometimes talks about the otherness of God, and Naughty Nora's most endearing quality is her otherness. Often, she will make the right choice but the grown-ups around her are too worldly-wise to see it and they just assume that she is up to no good again. This is what appeals to children the most.

We were sad when the Cottrell family and Naughty Nora left us and, although we tried to remember the stories we had been told, they never seemed to sound quite the same. I am therefore delighted that Bishop Stephen has published a book of her stories.

So welcome back, Naughty Nora! There is a whole new generation of children waiting to listen to your adventures.

Sue Drake, former head teacher, Lindley CE (VA) Infant School, Huddersfield

Introduction

Naughty Nora is the naughtiest girl in her school.

There is a little bit of naughtiness inside everybody, but just imagine taking all those little bits of naughtiness and putting them inside one person! Well, that gives you some idea of how naughty Naughty Nora is. She is *very* naughty indeed.

But, like many naughty people, as well as getting into trouble, Naughty Nora knows how to say 'sorry'. She knows about fun, forgiveness, mischief, joy and grace. This book is the story of her adventures.

How to use this book

Stories are a vitally important way of communicating Christian faith. Jesus told stories, and the intention behind the stories about Naughty Nora is that (in a similar way to the parables we find in the Bible) they will encourage children to think through the ideas and make connections to their own experiences of school, home and the teaching of the Christian faith.

At the end of each story, there are suggested questions and Bible references that can help the storyteller to lead the children into a deeper understanding of the story and to encourage them to question and explore it. First of all, though, a story is just that—a story. It is to be read and enjoyed.

I imagine these stories being used in a number of different ways, as outlined overleaf.

In collective worship

Most of the stories in this book began life as school assemblies. This book can therefore be used as a resource book for schools. However, I don't imagine the stories just being read out. Rather, I hope that whoever uses this book will have the courage to retell the story. This takes a bit of practice and a lot of nerve, but I think that most people can do it. Once we have the basic plot inside our head, we can retell a story to others. In this way, I hope that teachers, clergy and others who regularly go into schools to lead collective worship will be inspired by these stories and then make them their own.

At the end of each story, there is a short section headed 'Retelling the story'. This gives a few tips, particularly on the use of props. Most of all, though, you just need to get the story into your head and rehearse it a few times at home—preferably with someone else listening and prompting. A story being told works much better than a story read out in the context of an assembly. It leaves the storyteller free to add their own ideas and other points of local detail that will bring the story even more to life.

The questions to explore with children, biblical references and parallels can be used; there is also a prayer that can be said. All this can be woven into the collective worship in whatever way seems appropriate.

In the classroom

Most primary schools have a time each day—perhaps as part of Literacy Hour—when the children gather on the carpet and a story is read. Naughty Nora's adventures and the questions that can be explored with the children afterwards make a perfect way of using this time. In this context, the stories are better read out than retold.

Other contexts

As well as retelling these stories in assemblies, I have field-tested them all on my own children, reading them aloud at home. Children love having stories read to them. This book is just as relevant for the home as it is for school—either for children to read themselves or for parents to read with them.

All that was said for collective worship above is also true for family services in church. These stories can be retold as part of worship. Many of the stories relate to themes and seasons in the Church year, so Naughty Nora could become a regular visitor at family worship.

At the moment, there is a huge interest in reflective storytelling. Its emphasis on exploring faith through story encourages a sense of wonder and invites children to explore stories through questions, discussion and creative exploration. This collection of stories supports this approach to ministry with children.

Chapter 1

Naughty Nora cleans up

Nora Grace is the naughtiest little girl for miles around.

She lives with her mum and dad, her little brother Nat, and their pet cat Pickles, in a small house on the edge of town. She is nine years old, with pigtails and dark brown eyes.

She likes football, loud music, dancing and getting into mischief. She always has a twinkle in her eye. She is always hatching exciting plans. She is quite a handful.

Nora doesn't mean to get into trouble, but she often does. She is one of those people who are fun to be around. She tries to fill every moment of every day with as much adventure as possible, but she doesn't always think carefully about what she is going to do before she does it. At school and at home everyone knows her as 'Naughty Nora'.

On Saturday mornings, Nora and Nat usually play football. They come home tired and happy and covered in mud. But on this particular Saturday—and not for the first time—Nora trudged into the house without taking her boots off.

'Nora!' screamed Mum, coming in behind her.

'Oh, sorry, Mum,' said Nora, looking at the trail of muddy footprints following her across the hall.

'Clear this up, please,' said Mum.

So Nora spent the next ten minutes cleaning the carpet in the hall.

'And now go and clean yourself!' said Mum.

So Nora spent the next twenty minutes in the bathroom,

and when she came downstairs she was squeaky clean.

'That's better,' said Mum. 'Now please try not to make any more mess today.'

Later in the morning, Nora made herself a large bowl of cereal. She dribbled some honey and a dollop of gooseberry jam over the top. (I forgot to tell you: Naughty Nora does have very strange taste in food.)

She went into the sitting room and started tucking into her cereal hungrily, but then she and Nat got into an argument— like brothers and sisters often do. Nat said that Nora was sitting in his chair, and she said that the chairs belonged to everybody. Then, with the bowl of cereal still on her lap, she reached out to give Nat a good poke. Nat pushed back at her and all of a sudden the bowl of cereal wasn't on her lap any more, but flying through the air, and gooseberry jam and honey-coated cornflakes were raining down on the carpet. Some landed on Nat, and he ran out of the room, screaming. Some landed on the cat, and she went and hid under the settee. There were quite a few flakes plastered across the television screen... and some on the wall.

Nora was amazed. Could there really have been that many cornflakes in the bowl? The room seemed to be covered in them.

One flake that Nora didn't notice had landed on the lampshade hanging from the centre of the ceiling. When Dad came into the room to see what the noise was about, he found Nora down on her knees, picking cornflakes out of the carpet.

'What on earth is going on in here?' he cried.

'Cornflakes,' said Nora. 'Bit of a disaster. I'm clearing it up.'

'I should think so,' said Dad. But at that moment the cornflake on the lampshade fell off and, fluttering downwards, landed on his bald patch.

Nora knew she shouldn't laugh. She knew she should really be looking solemn and serious. But she couldn't help it. There are some things you just have to laugh at, whatever the consequences. Dad looked so funny with a large glob of sticky cornflakes on his head. So Naughty Nora spent the rest of the morning in her bedroom.

Mum came to fetch her at lunch time. 'Will you *please* behave nicely,' she said. 'And *please* be more careful. And *please*, no more mess.'

In the afternoon, Nora decided to take herself off on her own. Nat had a friend round and they were playing upstairs. Mum was doing some gardening out the back. Dad was in the kitchen, surrounded by pots and pans, cooking up a feast for tea. He didn't want to be disturbed. He was wearing his 'please do not disturb me' face.

Nora went round to the garage. For some while she had been planning to do something to her bike. It was just an ordinary, fairly boring bike at the moment. She wanted to paint it... and put mirrors and stickers on it... and maybe fly a flag from the back mudguard... or get some really big handlebars... and a bell—or, even better, a horn.

She stood looking at her bike, dreaming of the super-bike she hoped it would become. Well, maybe she could get started this afternoon. There was nothing else to do.

She rummaged about among Dad's pots of paint. At the back was a tin of black enamel paint. 'Just the thing for a bike,' thought Nora. Jet black was the perfect colour.

She carefully opened the tin and gave the paint a stir with a piece of stick. It seemed OK, and the tin was nearly full. She felt sure that Dad wouldn't mind if she borrowed it.

She wheeled her bike on to the front drive, turned it upside down so that it was resting securely on its handlebars, and started painting. Pickles, the cat, wandered out of the house and came and sat on the wall to watch. Before long, most of the metalwork was painted and the bike was gleaming black.

But some of the paint was dripping on to the drive. Nora didn't notice it at first. She should have put down some newspaper before she started, or an old sheet, but in her enthusiasm she hadn't thought of this. When she did see the mess she was making, instead of thinking calmly about how to clear it up, she panicked. She had been kneeling down, and she quickly jumped up.

'Oh, goodness!' she said. 'I must do something.'

But as she jumped up, Nora lost her balance. Taking a step backwards, she put her foot right into the tin of paint. Taking a step forwards, she bumped straight into the bike. The bike fell one way, and Nora fell the other, and the paint went everywhere. When she looked around, there was a puddle of black paint in the middle of the drive, and splatters of black paint all around her and all over her.

She ran to the house to get something to clean up the mess and, for the second time that day, she was leaving a trail of dirty footprints. This time, though, it wasn't mud, which was easy to clean up, but paint. Just as Nora was opening the front door to go in, Mum came round the side of the house. She saw the mess on the drive. She saw the footprints. She saw Naughty Nora about to go indoors.

'STOP!' she shouted. 'Do not take another step. Stand

absolutely still. Do not move a muscle. Do not even breathe.'

Nora froze on the doorstep.

'Now, turn round really slowly, and try not to move your feet more than you have to.'

Nora slowly turned around. It was then that she saw that her shoes were covered in black paint.

'Oh, lummy,' she said.

Mum was about to say something else when Pickles, who had just padded through the puddle of paint herself, gave a loud 'Meow' and jumped up into Mum's arms. Mum was covered with black enamel paint pawprints.

'This really is the limit,' said Mum. 'Nora, roll up your sleeves: you've got some cleaning to do!'

But this mess was too big for Nora to clear up on her own. So, after she had said how sorry she was, and promised that she would always be more careful in the future, and after she had checked that her bike was OK and explained to Dad her plans for it, both she and Mum spent the next hour cleaning and scrubbing the front drive and the porch.

The porch was already quite dirty and hadn't been cleaned for ages. As Nora and Mum scrubbed away, they both calmed down and they even began to enjoy themselves. 'This step needs a good clean,' said Mum.

They also noticed that beneath the paint, and beneath the dirt, there was some sort of pattern to the stones, and some of them even seemed to be a slightly different colour and made of a different material.

'This is interesting,' said Nora.

'Yes,' said Mum. 'Let's keep scrubbing away and see what we find.'

As they cleaned, more of the pattern was revealed, and in between the stones there were thin, rusty red strips of what seemed to be brick or tile. By the time they'd finished, the front porch looked as good as new, and the step was shown to be made up of different stones and pieces of brick laid out in a criss-cross pattern. They had never seen the pattern before. Dad and Nat came out, and they all stood and admired their new front step. It looked really nice.

'So some good came out of my naughtiness today,' said Nora as she was getting into bed.

'I suppose so,' said Mum. 'Now get some sleep; we've had a most eventful day.'

Nora looked up at her mum as she turned out the bedroom light.

'Washing isn't just about getting rid of dirt, is it, Mum?'

Mum thought for a bit.

'You're right. Cleaning something shows you what's really there. When you had that shower this morning, it wasn't just to get rid of the mud. It was so that we could see the beautiful you, all squeaky and clean.'

'And the step this afternoon,' said Nora. 'We never realized how pretty it was until we cleaned it.'

Mum came over to give Nora a last kiss goodnight and Nora stretched up to hug her mum. As she did so, her elbow caught the edge of the bedside table. On it was her glass of water. It tumbled sideways, splashing all over Mum's feet.

Nora and Mum looked at each other. Neither of them said a word.

'Oh dear,' said Nora, eventually. 'Still, perhaps they needed a clean. Now we'll be able to discover what beautiful feet you've got!'

Mum stared at Nora for another moment with a cross look on her face, but it soon melted into a smile.

'You are without doubt the most exasperating person I know!'

Questions to explore with children

Have you ever cleaned something and discovered that it was more beautiful than you realized? Have you ever got into trouble making a mess, like Naughty Nora, and had to clean it up? I wonder how it feels to discover something really beautiful?

 ## Jesus says...

'Love each other, as I have loved you.'
JOHN 15:12

It is God's love for us in Jesus that makes us clean and whole. It is our love for each other that can bring healing and peace to the world.

In the Bible there are stories about Jesus cleaning, washing and healing people, and revealing how beautiful they are to God. He washes his disciples' feet (John 13:5) and gives them the 'new commandment' to love one another (15:12). He heals ten lepers, but only one comes back to say 'thank you' (Luke 17:11–19). A woman washes Jesus' feet with her tears (Luke 7:36–50). He says that she must have been forgiven a lot because she loves so much.

 ## Prayer

Caring God,
wash me through and through
so that I can become the beautiful person
I am meant to be. Amen

 ## Retelling the story

Showing a picture of dirty footprints, or even making some footprints on the floor (as long as they can easily be cleaned afterwards!) would be one way of bringing this story to life.

Chapter 2

Naughty Nora discovers the importance of listening

Naughty Nora goes to St Wilfrid's school, which is near where she lives. Most mornings she catches the bus from the end of her road, but some mornings she is late (usually because she has been naughty) and her mum or dad has to take her in the car.

Nora's teacher is called Mrs Watkins. When Mrs Watkins heard that Naughty Nora was going to be in her class, she gave a big sigh. Naughty Nora is probably the naughtiest person who has ever been to St Wilfrid's school.

Nora has lots of friends. In particular, she likes to play with Gary Wild, who is a boy after her own heart, but there are lots of others. Naughty Nora is a fun person to be with—but having fun is one thing; not doing as you're told is another. In lesson times, when she was supposed to be busy working, Nora was often busy doing something else. Usually it was chatting. Nora was probably the worst chatterbox the school had ever known. Mrs Watkins said that if she had ten pence for every time she had asked Nora to be quiet, she would be a millionaire.

When everyone was asked to sit at their tables at the beginning of the day for the register, Naughty Nora would usually be chatting.

When Mrs Watkins was explaining the work they were

going to be doing that day, Naughty Nora would usually be chatting.

When the rest of the class (or, at least, most of them) were quietly getting on with their work, Naughty Nora would be whispering to the person next to her about something completely different.

When everyone sat on the carpet at the end of the day for a story… well, you've guessed it, every few minutes Mrs Watkins had to stop reading the story and ask Nora to be quiet.

If Naughty Nora wasn't chatting, she was dreaming. She was the worst daydreamer in the class. It was all or nothing with her: she was either chattering away ten to the dozen, annoying or entertaining the children around her, or she was staring out of the window, thinking about something else and not paying any attention to what the teacher was saying.

One morning, a few weeks after the beginning of term, Mrs Watkins asked everyone in the class to sit up straight and be quiet because she had an important announcement to make.

'So do I,' whispered Nora to Gary Wild, who was sitting next to her. 'I've got to announce that I have found the tree with the most conkers on it. It's just round the corner from the school.'

She opened her pocket to show Gary the conkers she had collected that morning.

'There are hundreds, and they're just starting to fall. If we go there after school and chuck some sticks up into the branches, I bet we can get loads.'

Meanwhile, Mrs Watkins was carrying on with her announcement, and Nora wasn't listening to a word she was saying.

At the end of the day, after a story had been read, Mrs

Watkins reminded everyone in the class not to forget what she had told them in the morning. But this time Nora wasn't chatting, she was dreaming. From her seat by the window she could see the conker tree, and she was imagining picking up the bright, shiny conkers.

As soon as the bell rang, she was out of the classroom in a flash. She never noticed all the other children collecting a piece of paper from Mrs Watkins' desk, and Mrs Watkins had a cross look on her face.

The following week, Mrs Watkins again had an announcement to make. She started off by saying, 'I hope you have all remembered what is happening tomorrow...' But again Naughty Nora wasn't listening. This time she was chatting to Amanda Goodchild.

Amanda Goodchild is the goodest girl in the school. No two children could be as different from each other as Amanda Goodchild and Nora Grace. Actually, though, despite the fact that they often annoyed each other, they were quite good friends. Nora, in that naughty way of hers, quite liked trying to get Amanda into trouble by talking to her when everyone was supposed to be quiet.

'Look at these conkers!' said Nora. 'If you let me copy your spellings when Mrs Watkins gives us a test this week, I'll let you have one conker for each spelling I get right.'

'Don't be so silly!' said Amanda. 'And anyway, that would be cheating.'

'I'm only teasing you,' said Nora. 'Would you like some?'

'Later,' said Amanda Goodchild. 'I'm trying to listen to Mrs Watkins.'

'Quiet in the back there,' said Mrs Watkins. 'Is that you talking, Amanda? I expected better behaviour from you.'

Amanda Goodchild went bright red. She hated being told off, and she turned and scowled at Naughty Nora, who had a big grin on her face.

'I might have guessed,' said Mrs Watkins. 'Nora Grace, have you been listening to a word I've said?'

'Yes, Miss. Of course, Miss,' said Nora, but this was a fib. Naughty Nora hadn't heard any of it at all.

'Well, perhaps you'd like to tell the class what I've just been saying,' continued Mrs Watkins.

Nora gulped. She hadn't been listening, but she knew it was something to do with tomorrow. She made a wild guess. 'About tomorrow, Miss. You've been telling us about all the important arrangements for tomorrow...'

Mrs Watkins frowned. 'So you are clear about all the arrangements, are you?'

'Oh yes, Miss. Very clear,' said Nora.

Mrs Watkins frowned again and then turned to the class.

'Does anyone else have any questions?' she said.

There was silence.

'OK, then, we are all set.'

With that, the class was dismissed and Nora heaved a sigh of relief. It had been a narrow escape.

That evening, while Dad was cooking tea, the telephone rang. Nora answered it and, to her surprise, it was Mrs Watkins.

'Is your mother home?' asked Mrs Watkins.

Nora gingerly handed the phone to Mum. What on earth was going on?

'I think you had better leave the room,' said Mum to Nora. 'This is going to be a private conversation.'

Nora left the kitchen but she made sure the door wasn't quite closed. Checking that Nat was nowhere to be seen, she pressed her ear against the door, and this is what she heard her mum saying...

'Oh, yes, Mrs Watkins... Of course, Mrs Watkins... Very good idea, Mrs Watkins... I'm sure it will do the trick, Mrs Watkins... I'll see you in the morning, Mrs Watkins.'

None of it made any sense. When Mum put the phone down, Nora didn't go back into the kitchen straight away. Over tea she quizzed Mum about what Mrs Watkins had wanted, but Mum only said it was something to do with school and nothing for Nora to worry about.

The next morning, Naughty Nora went to school as usual, but when she got to school, things were very far from usual. First of all, when she arrived in the playground (her pockets stuffed with conkers), she looked around for some of her friends to play with, but none of them were there. 'That's funny,' she thought. 'Where can they be? Everyone seems to be late this morning.'

When the bell rang for school to begin, everyone lined up in their different classes and were led into school by their teachers. But not only was Naughty Nora the only person from her class in the playground; Mrs Watkins wasn't there either.

All the other classes filed into school and Naughty Nora didn't know what to do. After a few minutes, she just tagged along after the last class. She went into her classroom, wondering whether everyone might already be there for some reason, but it was empty. Naughty Nora started to feel anxious. Something was wrong. Where could everyone be? Where was Mrs Watkins?

She waited a few more minutes, but just as she had decided to go and find another teacher, the door of the classroom burst open and someone came in. It wasn't the person she was expecting to see. It was Mum, and behind Mum was Mrs Watkins, and behind Mrs Watkins was Mrs Starling, the head teacher.

'Have you forgotten something?' said Mum.

'Err, I don't think so,' said Naughty Nora.

'Are you sure?' said Mrs Starling.

'What about the important thing that is happening today? Are you sure about all of that?' said Mrs Watkins.

Naughty Nora's face fell. She knew she had done something wrong, but she didn't know what it was. She decided it was time to own up.

'You know I said I was clear about the arrangements for today?' said Nora. 'Well, that might have been a slight exaggeration...'

'An exaggeration, my foot,' said Mrs Watkins. 'I don't think you were listening to a word I was saying. Today is the day that we are all going on a school trip. We are going to London, to the Science Museum and then on to St Paul's Cathedral. If you had been listening, you would have known. Everyone else in the class is already on the coach outside, because everyone else listened to what I was saying last week. Everyone else took home the information sheet for parents that I gave them, and brought the consent forms back again, and remembered to meet ten minutes early at the back of the school, where the coach is waiting!'

Naughty Nora was distraught. 'Have I missed the trip?'

'No,' said Mrs Watkins, kindly. 'The coach is waiting. But I knew that you hadn't been listening, so I spoke to your mother last night on the telephone, and we thought this might teach you a lesson.'

Nora looked relieved. 'I'm sorry, Mrs Watkins,' she said. 'I'm sorry, Mum. I'm sorry, Mrs Starling. I have learned a lesson. I really will try to listen more in the future.'

'And chatter a bit less,' added the head teacher.

Mum gave her a hug and told her how much she loved her, even though she could sometimes be very naughty. Nora got on the coach with the rest of her friends, who all cheered when she appeared.

'I've been a twit,' she said.

On the way home, after a lovely day out, Mrs Watkins sat down next to Nora for a bit.

'Nora, I do hope you have learnt your lesson,' she said. 'It really is important to listen and pay attention. You don't want this sort of thing to happen again.'

But Nora was staring out of the coach window, dreaming about growing up to be a scientist, or perhaps the Dean of St Paul's Cathedral.

'Oh, sorry, Mrs Watkins,' she said. 'Did you say something?'

Questions to explore with children

Can you remember ever getting into trouble because you weren't listening properly? Does your mum or your teacher sometimes have to remind you to pay attention? How does it feel if someone isn't listening to you, or if someone ignores you? I wonder how Naughty Nora felt when she thought she had missed the trip?

 ## Jesus says...

'If you have ears, pay attention.'
MARK 4:9

We will never learn if we never listen. We've got two ears and only one mouth. That's because listening is so important. We need to listen to God as we hear him speak to us through the stories of the Bible. We need to listen to each other. We need to listen to those who love us and care for us. Jesus also tells us that God listens to us. 'Ask, and you will receive,' says Jesus (Matthew 7:7).

In the part of the Bible called the Old Testament, there is a lovely story about a boy called Samuel who hears God calling him. At first, he doesn't realize it is God speaking, but eventually he learns to listen for God's voice (1 Samuel 3:1–19).

 ## Prayer

Patient God,
thank you for listening to our prayers.
Help us to listen to you and to each other. Amen

 ## Retelling the story

This story really just needs telling, although a pocket full of conkers will help illustrate the relevant part of the story.

Chapter 3

A most unusual harvest festival

Naughty Nora was very excited. At school they were going to
have a harvest festival as a way of saying 'thank you' to God
for all the good things they enjoyed. There was going to be a
special assembly, and Sue, the priest from their church, was
going to be there.

Everyone in the class had been asked to bring something in.
It could be some fresh fruit or vegetables, or it could be tinned
food. Both were needed. In the afternoon, all the produce that
had been collected was going to be taken to the shelter nearby,
where homeless people could stay and get something to eat.

Naughty Nora wondered what she could bring.

'I've grown some beetroot on my grandad's allotment,' said
Gary Wild. 'I'll bring that in.'

'Marvellous!' said Mrs Watkins. 'Let's hope the people at
the shelter like beetroot.'

'My dad is a greengrocer,' said Junji. 'I'm sure he would give
us lots of stuff.'

'Excellent!' said Mrs Watkins. 'We're halfway there already.'

On the day of the harvest assembly, Naughty Nora woke up
early.

Dad was still in bed. She could hear faint snores coming
from her parents' bedroom. Nat was also asleep.

Mum was on the landing in her dressing-gown, about to go into the shower.

'It's harvest festival today,' said Nora. 'I need to take something into school.'

'I'll find you something when I come down,' said Mum, yawning. 'I'm just going to wash my hair.'

Mum disappeared into the bathroom and Nora hurried downstairs. 'I don't need to wait till Mum comes down,' she thought. 'I can sort some things out now. It will save time.'

She knelt down in front of the fridge and opened the door. There were lots of good things she could take—milk, butter, eggs, jam. One by one, she took them out of the fridge and laid them on the floor by her side.

'Now then, what else?' she said to herself.

There were some bananas in the fruit bowl. 'I can get those later,' she thought. 'I wonder if homeless people like Marmite.'

She went over to the cupboard to see if there was some Marmite she could take. Sure enough, there was a new jar at the back. Now all she needed was a bag to put everything in.

Naughty Nora was standing in the kitchen thinking about this when Mum came downstairs from her shower. She was still in her dressing-gown and, as she was drying her hair, she had a towel wrapped round her head. It had slipped a little so that it was half covering her eyes, and she was slightly distracted, thinking about something else.

Mum wasn't expecting a dish of butter to be on the kitchen floor just inside the door. She stepped into the room and... Oh no! Her bare right foot trod on top of the butter. She gave a surprised yelp and slid across the kitchen floor, knocking over the milk as she went.

Steadying herself, she grabbed hold of the kitchen work-top and sent the fruit bowl flying into the air. Her left foot stepped into the eggs, and her right foot (still coated in butter) knocked into the jam pot, which rolled into the wall and smashed at just about the same time that the fruit bowl fell to the floor with a crash.

Mum herself came to an abrupt halt as she slammed into the back door, knocking over the broom. It fell on to some china that was on the draining-board. Several cups and plates cascaded to the floor, smashing one at a time as they fell. Meanwhile, the bananas had landed—one of them half floating in the middle of a growing puddle of milk and egg.

'Oh lummy,' said Nora, and dropped the Marmite.

It was then that Dad came downstairs. He stood in the kitchen doorway and surveyed the scene.

In front of him was a large puddle of milk and broken eggs. Then there was a little pile of broken china. Beyond that was a smashed bowl and a little mound of strawberry jam and broken glass. The broom was in the sink. Mum had a towel over her head and her face was pressed against the back door. It looked as if she had half a pound of butter stuck to her foot.

Nora was on the other side of the kitchen. In front of her was a black, sticky puddle of goodness-knows-what.

'I can explain everything,' said Nora, stepping forward into the Marmite. As she walked towards Dad, she made big black footprints on the kitchen floor.

Well, I can hardly tell you what happened next. Naughty Nora was in big trouble. It had been an accident. It was unfortunate that Mum hadn't seen the food on the floor, but it was very silly of Nora to put it there in the first place. The only person who enjoyed it was Pickles, who quietly padded into the kitchen and licked up the milk and egg.

First of all, Nora was sent to her room. Then she was

summoned back down again to help clear up. Then she said she was sorry, and when Mum and Dad had calmed down everyone was able to laugh about what had happened. But Dad was late for work, and by the time everything was back to normal Nora and Nat were getting late for school. Nora hadn't even had any breakfast.

They left the house just in time to catch the bus to school from the end of the road. But as Nora was about to get on to the bus, she realized with horror that she had forgotten to bring anything for the harvest festival.

She rushed back home. Mum was in the kitchen giving the floor another clean. (Marmite isn't easy to get rid of.)

'Mum,' said Nora, frantically, 'I haven't got anything to take to school for harvest.'

On the worktop were two sad-looking bananas, left over from the morning's escapades.

'Take these,' said Mum with a sigh. She put them in a bag and Nora left for school.

Having missed the bus, Nora would normally have asked Mum for a lift, but she had already caused enough trouble so she decided to walk. On top of everything, she would now be late for school.

Naughty Nora trudged along the road, feeling sorry for herself. She hadn't meant to cause all those problems. Now all she had for the harvest were these two bananas, and she had missed breakfast. She hated missing breakfast. 'Breakfast is the most important meal of the day,' she thought to herself.

Nora took the bananas out of the bag and looked at them. What a pathetic offering! One looked very bruised, and as she looked at them, her stomach rumbled.

She stopped. Would taking just one banana to school be much worse than taking two? This bruised banana wasn't really good enough for the harvest festival... though it might be all right on the inside.

She slowly peeled back the skin from the top of the banana. It looked fine. But now, of course, it was open. She couldn't take it in like that. It would be rude.

She lifted the banana to her lips. 'I've still got the other one,' she said to herself, and, without another thought, she started eating. The banana was delicious.

Nora walked on a bit further, feeling slightly guilty—but she still had one banana.

But she was also still hungry, and now she was thinking that maybe it was better to tell Mrs Watkins that she had forgotten to bring anything than to offer this one sad-looking banana. No sooner had she thought this than she found herself greedily devouring the second banana as well.

When she arrived at the school gates, instead of a harvest offering she was holding a brown paper bag containing two banana skins.

It was also just her bad luck that the head teacher had chosen that morning to stand at the school gates and check on latecomers.

'I might have guessed,' said Mrs Starling, with a face that looked like thunder. 'Nora Grace: late for school!'

She marched Nora into the school and stood her outside her office, just next to the hall. 'I'll deal with you later,' she said. 'Right now I've got to get everything ready for the harvest assembly. At least I see you've brought something with you. Now let me have your offering and I'll put it on the display with everything else.'

It was at this moment that an already bad morning got much, much worse.

'A harvest offering?' said Nora, trying to hide the bag behind her back. 'Oh no, Mrs Starling, this isn't a harvest offering. I forgot my harvest gift. This is just an old bag.'

'Don't be so silly, girl. Of course it's your harvest offering! Now give it to me and I'll put it with the others.'

Nora's heart sank. There was no way out. She handed the bag to Mrs Starling and hung her head in shame.

Well, you can probably imagine what happened next. When Mrs Starling saw the banana skins, she was furious. But there wasn't time to deal with Naughty Nora because, at that very moment, Sue, the priest, came through the door with a cheery smile on her face.

Mrs Starling hissed under her breath that she would really, *really* deal with Nora this time, but actually left her standing outside the hall as she went off with Sue.

Nora was all alone.

It had been a terrible morning. Everything that could go wrong had gone wrong.

She felt awful. She wished there was something she could do to put things right.

She looked into the hall and saw the beautiful display of harvest goods: cabbages, carrots, pumpkins, marrows, with lots of tins and packets alongside them—different things to say 'thank you' to God for the wonderful provision that we have. And at the side of the hall were some cardboard boxes, ready for the food to be put in and taken to the homeless shelter. Nora had an idea…

When it was time for the assembly to begin, all the pupils filed into the hall. The smallest children from Reception sat at the front, and the oldest children in Year 6 sat on benches at the back. Mrs Watkins led in Naughty Nora's class. They all sat down but, of course, Nora herself wasn't there. The teachers sat around the edge of the hall. Some mums and dads had also come along and were sitting at the back. At the front were Sue and Mrs Starling.

Everyone was looking at the beautiful display of food, and everyone was having the same thought. Everyone was thinking, 'Who put that cardboard box in the middle of the display?' For right in the middle of all the vegetables was a big cardboard box.

Mrs Starling thought Sue must have put it there as part of her talk—a sort of visual aid. Sue thought Mrs Starling must have put it there, and I suppose everyone else just thought that it was part of the assembly, but it did look a bit funny.

Gary Wild nudged Amanda Goodchild in the ribs and whispered, 'Who put that cardboard box there?' Amanda Goodchild looked stuffily down her nose at Gary and told him to be quiet. Then Mrs Watkins said 'Shhhhh' to them both, and Amanda went bright red because she never got told off. At last the assembly began.

First of all, there was a song about fluffy cauliflowers and not forgetting to give thanks. It was a song that everyone loved. Then Sue told a story about being thankful for the food we have and for those who made it, and about sharing what we have with others. She said that the food that was brought in for the assembly was a sign of our thankfulness. Then Mrs Starling told everyone about the homelessness shelter and what would happen to the food. Sue said a prayer, and there was a final song. And everyone was still thinking, 'What is that cardboard box doing in the middle of the display?'

After the song had finished, everyone found out, for just as

Sue was standing up to give a blessing, the cardboard box opened and Naughty Nora stood up.

Everyone gasped.

Mrs Watkins' glasses fell off her nose. Mrs Starling's face went as red as Gary Wild's beetroot.

Sue, however, had a big smile on her face. 'Well, goodness me,' she said. 'What have we here?'

There was silence in the hall. You could have heard a pin drop. Then Naughty Nora spoke up.

'It's a harvest offering,' she said. 'I forgot to bring something this morning. Well, that's not quite true. I got into trouble at home and nearly forgot to bring something. But I missed my breakfast and I missed the bus, and on the way to school... well, I ate the bananas I was supposed to bring in. I don't know why I did it. I'm really sorry, and I've been really stupid, but I love harvest and I did want to offer something, so I've decided to offer myself. And if it will make things better, I'd like to help pack up the stuff that everyone else has brought in and take it to the shelter after school.'

There was still silence in the hall. No one could quite believe their eyes and ears. Then Sue spoke.

'What a brilliant idea. I'm sure Mrs Starling would love to take you up on that offer, wouldn't you, Mrs Starling?'

'Err, yes, yes, of course,' said the head teacher. And with that everyone started clapping.

It was the most unusual harvest gift, but in many ways it was the best.

Questions to explore with children

Can you remember what you brought to harvest festival last year? I wonder what everyone was thinking when they saw Naughty Nora appear out of the cardboard box? I wonder how Naughty Nora felt when she ate the bananas and got into trouble and realized she had nothing to offer?

 ## Jesus says...

'Even the hairs on your head are counted.'
MATTHEW 10:30

Naughty Nora shouldn't have eaten the bananas, but in many ways she was right. The best gift we can offer God is ourselves.

In the Bible there are lots of stories about sharing—like the one about the small boy who shares his lunch with Jesus. Jesus feeds five thousand people with it! (John 6:1–14).

 ## Prayer

Generous God,
we thank you for all the good things we enjoy.
Help us to share them with others,
and help us to offer you the best gift of all—ourselves! Amen

 ## Retelling the story

Props will help with this story. Produce some bananas—which you could eat yourself as you tell the story—or at least a bag with some banana skins in it. A big cardboard box and other harvest gifts will also be useful.

Chapter 4

Naughty Nora discovers how fibs grow

Naughty Nora was feeling very worried. She had not done her homework. Mrs Watkins had asked her whole class to write a poem over the weekend. The poem was supposed to be about something you had learnt recently—like your six times table, or how to do up your shoelaces, or how to stand on your head. Nora couldn't do any of these things. (Well, she could stand on her head, but she hadn't learnt that recently; she had always been able to do it.)

'Anything will do,' Mrs Watkins had said in her cheery way, but Nora couldn't think of anything, and then, when the weekend came, she was much too busy having fun to think about writing a poem. She hadn't written it down in her homework diary, like she was supposed to do, so when her mum asked her if she had any homework, she said, 'No'.

It was only a little fib. 'Little fibs don't do any harm,' thought Nora. She would do the homework—but when she wanted to.

If she told Mum she had homework, then Mum would just nag her all weekend. She would do it tomorrow, or get up early on Monday... but she forgot, and it was while she was on the bus to school on Monday morning that she suddenly remembered. But now it was too late.

'Oh lummy,' she thought, 'now I'll be in trouble. I will have to think of a plan—a really good plan, so that no one will suspect me of fibbing.' And this is what she did. As soon as school began, before Mrs Watkins had asked for the poems to be handed in, and before she had even called the register, Naughty Nora stuck up her hand—her left hand.

'Yes,' said Mrs Watkins, slowly, lowering the glasses on her nose so that she could get a better look at her most troublesome pupil.

'Mrs Watkins, excuse me, Mrs Watkins, but I'm very sorry, Mrs Watkins, but I'm afraid I couldn't write a poem over the weekend.'

'And why was that?' said Mrs Watkins, suspiciously.

'I hurt my hand,' said Naughty Nora. 'Mum said I shouldn't write with it… and so did the doctor, too.'

'Did they?' said Mrs Watkins, walking over to where Nora was sitting. 'Have you got a note from your mother about this?'

'Err, no,' said Nora, who had realized that the ever-vigilant Mrs Watkins would ask for a note and had her story ready. 'I did have a note but I've left it at home. I'll bring it in tomorrow.'

'Mmmmm. How convenient,' said Mrs Watkins. 'Let me have a look at this hand.'

All this time, Nora had kept her right hand under the desk. This was going to be the hardest part of her plan, because if it was really hurt then it would be bruised and bandaged and, of course, it wasn't. But Nora had thought of this, too, and was ready with her excuse.

'I'm afraid I can't move it,' she said. 'When I said my hand hurt, what I really should have said was that my whole arm hurt. I fell off the slide at the park and the doctor says I've bruised a nerve in my arm and so my whole arm has gone limp. You can't see any bruising and it doesn't need bandaging and it will be fine in a couple of days, but I can't move it at all. It just hangs down at my side.'

Nora pushed the desk forward with her left hand and showed Mrs Watkins her right arm hanging limp upon her lap. Mrs Watkins went to touch it and Nora yelped with pain.

'It's really tender,' she said.

Her cry was so convincing that even Mrs Watkins—who hadn't really believed Nora up till then—wondered if she might be telling the truth. After all, if it was a lie it was a very elaborate one.

So, for the rest of the morning, Naughty Nora didn't do any work, but sat and read and did a few things with her left hand and kept trying to remember not to use her right hand. She got lots of suspicious looks from her friends but inside she heaved a sigh of relief. She had got away with it! Now all she needed to do was forge a note from her mum (that shouldn't be too difficult) and then have a miraculous recovery in a couple of days. Meanwhile, although it was annoying not to be able to play at break-time, it was good not to have to do any work.

But after lunch, Mrs Watkins said to Nora, 'I'm rather worried about your arm. I think maybe you should be resting at home. I've decided to give your mother a ring and see if it wouldn't be better if you took the afternoon off.'

'Oh, don't do that,' said Nora. 'I mean, you can't do that. Mum isn't in.'

'Why not?' said Mrs Watkins. 'She's usually around in the afternoons.'

Nora didn't know what to say. She hadn't planned this bit of the story, so she said the first thing that came into her head. 'Mum's got a hospital appointment this afternoon.'

'Oh dear, a hospital appointment? I hope nothing's the matter.'

'Err... she fell over as well at the weekend. In fact, we were both going down the slide together. I fell off and hurt my arm and Mum bumped her head—really badly. She's going for an X-ray to check everything is all right. In fact...' (Nora was now warming to her theme) '... she seems to have lost her memory a bit. Even if you did speak to her, which you won't, because she's out, she probably wouldn't remember anything that happened. She's really confused. We're all really worried. She might even have to stay in hospital.'

'Nora, I am sorry,' said Mrs Watkins. 'You should have told me this morning. But don't worry; I'll phone your father. We have his number as well.'

'Oh no, don't do that. He's in Bulgaria!' said Nora.

She didn't know why she had said this. She was starting to panic, and somehow Bulgaria had flashed into her head. 'On work,' she added.

Mrs Watkins gave Nora a hard stare. 'I'll be back in a minute,' she said. 'Get on with your work quietly, Class 5.' She got up and left the room.

Poor Nora. She sat at her desk, sweating. All this over one fib. It just kept on growing. First of all, she'd said she had hurt her hand, and then that she had left the note at home. Then she had planned to forge a note tomorrow. Then she had said her mother had hurt herself as well, and then she had said her mother was in hospital. Then she had said her mother had lost her memory, and now she had said her dad was working in Bulgaria. That one little fib to get her out of trouble had grown and grown and was now about to get her into *huge* trouble.

The seconds ticked by. Everyone in the class was working

away; but from behind their books they were casting sneaky glances at Naughty Nora and sniggering under their breath. She was for it this time, they thought. She was bound to be fibbing.

After five minutes, Mrs Watkins came back into the class.

'Will your mother be picking you up as usual after school?' said Mrs Watkins in her cheery voice. 'When she returns from the hospital, of course.'

'Err, yes,' said Nora, slightly confused. She was expecting to be told off by Mrs Watkins. She thought she'd been found out. At this point, Gary Wild stood up.

'There's nothing wrong with Nora's hand, Miss. She's just putting it on to get out of work. It's not fair.'

'Do sit down, Gary,' said Mrs Watkins. 'We don't know anything of the sort. Nora has told us her hand is hurt and we must believe her. Now please, children, get on with your work.'

Nothing else was said about it all afternoon, and Nora thought that she *had* got away with it. 'Perhaps fibs work after all,' she thought.

When the bell rang for going home, Mrs Watkins smiled and called Nora over. 'Don't wait out in the cold with the other children. With your hand so poorly, we don't want you catching a chill or getting knocked into. Wait in here with me. Your mother will soon realize where you are and come and get you. I'll have a word with the teacher on the gate and she'll send her through.'

All the children left the class and Nora remained at her desk.

'Just find yourself a book to read,' said Mrs Watkins. 'I'm sure your mother will be along presently.'

Nora started reading. At first, she didn't think anything was up, but as the minutes ticked by, she started to get suspicious.

'I expect your mother has been delayed at the hospital. Don't worry, I've got some marking to do. I'm not in a hurry to get home.'

Five minutes ticked by. Ten minutes ticked by. Nora was getting worried—not worried that something had happened to her mum, as she was often a bit late—worried that her plan had not worked as well as she thought. It seemed as if Mrs Watkins knew something. Fifteen minutes went by.

'I think perhaps I'd better give the hospital a ring and see what's happened,' said Mrs Watkins, and left the room.

This was Naughty Nora's chance. She had to escape. She could tell Mrs Watkins in the morning that her mum had come while she was out of the room. She gathered her things together. She put on her coat. She gingerly poked her head out of the door of the classroom to check no one was about. She looked both ways. The coast was clear.

She hurried down the corridor as quickly and quietly as she could. She turned the corner towards the exit for the playground. She ran a little faster—nearly there. She opened the door into the playground. Free at last, and then.... CRASH! She bumped straight into Mrs Watkins, her mum and dad and the head teacher, who were coming the other way. She gasped and dropped her bag, and all her books fell on to the floor.

'Pick those up, dear,' said Mrs Watkins kindly.

Nora quickly scrabbled on her knees and started stuffing the books back into her bag... stuffing them in with both hands... stuffing them in with her right hand as well as her left hand.

'Wonderful,' said Mrs Watkins. 'A miraculous recovery… and Mr Grace, you're back from Bulgaria… and Mrs Grace, you seem to have got your memory back.'

'Yes,' said Naughty Nora's mum, sternly. 'I remember *everything* that happened last weekend.'

Naughty Nora hung her head in shame.

'Oh lummy,' she mumbled under her breath. She had been found out. How could she have been so stupid? When would she learn that one fib leads to another fib, and the fibs get bigger and more complicated and eventually you get found out? Even if you don't get found out, you still get trapped by all the confusion. It would be much better if you just told the truth in the first place.

Well, I won't tell you what happened next. Needless to say, Nora was in big trouble. She still had to write that poem about something she had learnt, and when she got home Mum sat her down and said there wouldn't be any tea until it was done. This is what she wrote:

A fib is like a little seed
That once it's planted grows so proud.
Its roots get deeper in the ground,
Its branches higher than a cloud.

You can't stop it growing high,
One ring fixes on another,
Till the little fib you told
Has led to many others.

One fib to excuse yourself
Is covered up by many more,
Until the truth itself is hid
And you don't know it any more.

So do not let the truth be hidden
By the fibs you sometimes tell.
Plant a seed of truth instead
And all things shall be well.

'Well done,' said Mrs Watkins when Nora handed her poem in. 'You've learnt something!'

Questions to explore with children

Can you remember a time when you told a fib and it got you into trouble? How did it feel? Did you get found out straight away, or did you have to tell another fib to cover up the first one?

We are all tempted to tell fibs, and all of us have told a fib at some time or another. Sometimes it seems hard to tell the truth because it means admitting we have done something wrong. But it is better to tell the truth and face the consequences than to make things worse by telling lies.

Jesus says...

'The truth will set you free.'
JOHN 8:32

What Jesus means is that, in the end, the truth comes out, and that truth is always better and stronger than lies. Even if we have done something wrong, it is better in the end to face up to it and be truthful, because then it can be sorted out.

In the Bible there are stories about people learning things the hard way. When Jesus is arrested, his friend Peter tells three lies—pretending he doesn't even know Jesus (Luke 22:56–61). He was worried that if he said he knew Jesus, he would get into trouble. After Jesus rises from the dead, he gives Peter another chance. Three times he says to Peter, 'Do you love me?'—one time for each of the fibs that Peter told (John 21:15–17).

Prayer

Truthful God,
help us to be truthful with you and with each other.
We are sorry for the times when we have told fibs.
Help us to learn from our mistakes. Amen

Retelling the story

This story is quite straightforward to retell. You can act out the bit where Nora shows the teacher her limp arm and the bit where she drops her bag and starts using both hands to pick up the books. You could read out the poem at the end.

Chapter 5

Naughty Nora discovers how not to get ready for Christmas

Christmas was only a few weeks away. Naughty Nora was getting excited. Naughty Nora was getting *very* excited. Naughty Nora was getting *too* excited. And you know how excitement sometimes turns to naughtiness. Well, that was what was happing to Nora. It seemed like she was in trouble all day at school. The teachers just didn't seem to understand that she couldn't help chatting when she was supposed to be quiet, fidgeting when she was supposed to be still. Didn't they know it was Christmas in a few weeks' time? Weren't they excited as well?

It was just as bad at home. One evening, Nora spilt her drink all over the new sofa while she was jumping up and down on it in excitement because some adverts had just come on the TV showing the new toy that she really wanted for Christmas. Somehow she had forgotten to put her drink down before jumping. It was a mistake anyone could make—but her mum didn't see it like that.

The next evening, she was helping her dad clean the dishes after tea and dropped a couple of plates. They smashed all over the floor into hundreds of pieces. It was only two plates. She couldn't see what all the fuss was about, and Dad didn't seem too pleased when Nora said that she was only practising her plate spinning, like she had seen at the circus. She was only joking, but Dad didn't see the funny side of it.

And then the next evening, worst of all, she tried to demonstrate to Nat how Father Christmas came down the chimney with a sack of presents, by jumping off the chest of drawers into the washing-up bowl. She borrowed her mum's new red coat to dress up as Father Christmas. It wasn't her fault that there was still some sticky gunk in the bottom of the bowl and the coat got stained. She had emptied the water out—well, most of it—and you could clean the coat. But Mum got really cross.

It didn't help that Nora slipped in the bowl and kicked Nat in the nose. Now he was sitting in the hall, bawling his eyes out and saying that Nora had beaten him up. She had done no such thing. It was an accident. It could happen to anyone —but it always seemed to happen to Nora. After tea she got sent up to her room to play on her own until bedtime.

Nora sat in her bedroom and sulked. She knew she'd been naughty, and now she felt quite sorry, but it was getting excited that had done it. She was just very excited about it being nearly Christmas.

While she sat in her bedroom, twiddling her thumbs and wondering what to do, she started thinking about what presents her mum and dad might have bought her for Christmas. They had been shopping recently and she had a good idea that they kept the presents on top of the wardrobe in their bedroom. In the past few weeks, Nora had spotted some bags and parcels beginning to appear and she had a feeling they were for her.

She tiptoed out of her bedroom on to the landing. She could hear Mum and Dad listening to the television downstairs. Nat was already asleep in his room. Very carefully, so that no one could hear, Nora opened the door to her parents' bedroom.

The door creaked as it opened and Nora held her breath, waiting to see if anyone had heard it. There was no sound of movement from downstairs.

She tiptoed in and switched on the light. There on top of the wardrobe were three or four bags bulging with... well, that was what Naughty Nora didn't know. Were they her presents? It was much too high up to see properly and she couldn't reach. And then it was that Naughty Nora did a very naughty thing—the naughtiest thing she had done all week.

'It wouldn't do any harm just to have a little peek,' she thought to herself. 'If I just get a chair from the landing and have the *tiniest* little look at what they've got, that wouldn't matter.'

So, getting the chair from the landing and placing it next to the wardrobe, she reached up. She could get her hand on to the top of the wardrobe, but it was a big, old wardrobe and the bags were stashed away right at the back. She felt around a bit, but still couldn't reach them.

Naughty Nora got a couple of big books to put on the chair. Still, she couldn't quite reach. She got another book. It was a bit wobbly. As she stood on the books, the chair started to move. But now, if she really stretched, she could just get hold of a corner of one of the bags.

'One more book will do it,' thought Nora. So, placing another book on the pile, she clambered up. Now the chair was very wobbly, and she climbed up gingerly. She still had to stretch, but now she could just get hold of a corner of the bag, pull it over to the edge of the wardrobe, and have a little look inside.

Her plan was working a treat, but then... disaster! One book slipped beneath her. She tried to keep her balance but the chair started to wobble. Her foot slid off the chair. The other books started to slide. Nora lunged out to grab the door handle of the wardrobe to break her fall, but it was too late... CRASH. She tumbled from the chair right on to her mum's dressing-table. As she fell, she knocked over a vase of flowers and, worse still, smashed one of her mother's favourite ornaments.

Naughty Nora lay on the floor, not daring to breathe. She was lying in a puddle of water from the spilt flowers. She was surrounded by the broken bits of china from the smashed ornament and, as she looked up, she could see a bag of presents wobbling on the top of the wardrobe. With another crash, they fell down on top of her.

They were her presents. She could see what they were now, but she was too embarrassed and worried to care. She quickly bundled them back into the bag. There was no noise from downstairs. She felt sure her parents must have heard the two crashes, but still no one came. She collected up the pieces of the broken ornament. She picked up the flowers and dabbed at the wet patch on the carpet with a towel.

'Oh lummy! Now what to do?' she thought to herself.

She knew that the right thing to do was to go downstairs and tell her mum and dad what had happened, but they were already cross with her. She was supposed to be in her bedroom. What would they say when they found out she had broken the ornament? And what would they say when they found out *how* she had broken the ornament? It was all too much. She just wanted to hide. She just wanted to pretend it hadn't happened.

Naughty Nora tidied up as best she could. She crept out of her parents' bedroom and tiptoed downstairs. She put on her coat and very quietly went out of the back door. Then she did another silly thing—she went and hid in the garage. She knew this was a silly thing to do. She knew that they would find out sooner or later what had happened, but she just felt so upset.

A little while later, Mum and Dad thought they would go and see Nora and tell her she could come down for a bit before bed. They went into her bedroom, but she wasn't there.

'That's strange,' said Dad. 'Where can she be?'

They looked in the bathroom, but Naughty Nora wasn't there. They looked in Nat's bedroom, but Naughty Nora wasn't there either. They looked in Nora's bedroom again. They went downstairs and looked in the kitchen, the dining room and the sitting room. They went back upstairs and looked in Nora's bedroom for a third time, this time shouting out, 'Nora! Nora, where are you? Stop hiding! Come out at once!'

But Nora was nowhere to be seen.

'Well, she can't just have disappeared,' said Mum, but it seemed as if that was exactly what had happened.

Then, they looked in their own bedroom, and as soon as they opened the door and saw the mess all over the floor, they guessed what had happened. Naughty Nora had been trying to look at the presents and had had an accident. They started searching the house once more. They looked all over but they just couldn't find her.

At last, something made Dad go into the garage. He kind of knew that Nora was hiding somewhere and he also knew that, although she was naughty, she would not be silly enough to actually run away. He went into the garage and heard a soft sobbing sound. Naughty Nora was sitting in the corner of the garage, huddled up in her coat, crying. Dad put his arms round her. He didn't say anything, he just held her tight. Then, after a little while, Nora spoke.

'I'm sorry, Dad,' she said.

'I know,' said Dad.

'I was trying to look at my presents,' said Nora.

'I know,' said Dad.

'I feel really silly.'

'I know,' said Dad.

'And I'm really sorry.'

'Well, that's good,' said Dad.

So Dad carried her inside and they had a warm drink. Mum and Dad had a cup of tea and Naughty Nora had hot lemon squash with ginger biscuits crumbled into it—a horrid combination but one of those things that Naughty Nora really loved.

'I just got excited,' said Nora after a while. 'And when I realized how silly I'd been, I just wanted to run away.'

Mum and Dad smiled. 'We forgive you,' they said.

'But don't go looking for your presents again,' said Dad.

'And no more Father Christmas impersonations,' said Mum.

There was another silence.

'Thank you for finding me,' said Naughty Nora.

Questions to explore with children

Have you ever felt like running away from something? Have you ever done anything silly and tried to cover it up, or pretend it wasn't you? I wonder how it feels to be lost?

Everybody makes mistakes sometimes, and all of us run away or feel like running away sometimes. God is on the look-out for us. We are all his children and he loves us very much.

Jesus says...

'I am the good shepherd. I know my sheep, and they know me.'
JOHN 10:14

In the Bible, there is the story of the prodigal son—someone who did silly things, ran away and was then found again (Luke 15:11–32). Then there are the stories of the lost sheep (Luke 15:1–7) and the lost coin (vv. 8–10), when someone who has lost something precious searches hard for it.

Prayer

Loving God,
thank you for Jesus,
who knows us better than we know ourselves
and searches for us when we run away.
Help us to forgive each other and to look out for one another,
today and every day. Amen

Retelling the story

This story can be retold quite easily and doesn't require any props, although it can be effective and dramatic to begin by showing everyone a smashed piece of china and going on to explain how it happened. In some circumstances, you could even break the china for everyone to see. This will certainly grab attention!

Chapter 6

Mrs Watkins has a bright idea

It was nearly Christmas. At Naughty Nora's school everyone was excited. They were getting ready for their nativity play. There was one problem, however. All the boys wanted to be Joseph and all the girls wanted to be Mary. Mrs Watkins didn't know what to do to keep everyone happy. Last year she had *one* happy Joseph and *one* happy Mary, three *fairly* happy kings, one *fairly* happy angel Gabriel, and lots and lots of very disgruntled shepherds and angels.

'We're going to need a narrator,' said Mrs Watkins. 'Now, that's a very important part. And the innkeeper and his wife—and King Herod—though, Gary, I don't think you can be King Herod this year. You rather frightened the little children with your threats last time.' (Gary had read around the subject and had taken to the part rather too enthusiastically.)

'Now, we can only have one Mary and one Joseph,' Mrs Watkins continued. 'I know that many of you will be upset, but the important thing is that we all pull together and we all play our part. Anyone who does not have a speaking part can be an angel or a shepherd and, of course, we can all sing the carols.'

Her voice trailed off. She could see the bored looks appearing on the faces of her class. She was really going to have to find a way of livening up this nativity play.

Amanda Goodchild put up her hand. 'Please, Miss, why don't you choose the most well-behaved boy and the most well-behaved girl, or the ones with the neatest handwriting, or the ones who have got the most gold stars this term?' She beamed at her teacher, for she knew full well that she herself came top in all these categories. Nora scowled at Amanda from across the room and muttered something unprintable under her breath.

'Thank you, Amanda, but I think I have a more ingenious way of selecting the parts for this year's play.'

Mrs Watkins asked all the children to write down on a piece of paper which character they would like to be in the nativity play, and to give a reason. She would then select the person who gave the best reason for wanting to play that part.

So, that morning, 13 boys sat down and wrote why they wanted to be Joseph, and 14 girls sat down and wrote why they wanted to be Mary. Some of the boys hedged their bets by saying that they also would be very happy to play a wise man, and some of the girls said that if they weren't chosen to be Mary they would very happily be the angel Gabriel.

They gave a variety of reasons as to why they should be chosen. Melanie said that she should be Mary because she had a blue dress. Tabita said that she should be Mary because her name meant 'graceful' and Mary was full of grace. David said that he should be Joseph because he dreamt a lot. Gary Wild said that he should be Joseph because he was the strongest boy in the class, and the fastest runner, and he could look after Mary the best and get them to Bethlehem in double-quick time.

Joseph said he should be Joseph because that was his name, and it would save getting in a muddle. Junji said that he would like to be Joseph, but he should definitely be a wise man because his mum and dad came from the east. Only one person said they wanted to be *anything* other than Mary or Joseph—and that person was Naughty Nora.

Naughty Nora didn't want to be Mary, and she certainly didn't want to be Joseph. She didn't want to be the angel Gabriel, and she didn't want to be a narrator. She didn't want to be an angel or a shepherd or a wise man (or one of the wise men's female assistants). No, she had another idea. She quickly wrote it down, folded her piece of paper in half and, while the rest of the class were dreaming up ever more strange and extravagant reasons for them to be chosen, she handed her piece of paper in.

That evening, and with a heavy heart, Mrs Watkins looked through all the pieces of paper. There were three piles—one pile of all the girls who wanted to be Mary, one pile of all the boys who wanted to be Joseph, and, all on its own, Naughty Nora's piece of paper.

Nora's piece of paper had given Mrs Watkins an idea. She went over to her computer and started writing. She wrote and she wrote and she wrote, and she sat up till after midnight, when, at last, she had finished the script for this year's nativity play.

When Mrs Watkins went into school the next morning, she had a spring in her step. As soon as she had called the register, she addressed her class.

'Children, last night, when I was looking through your reasons for wanting to be in the play, I had an idea. This year the nativity play is going to be rather different. No one is going to be Mary, and no one is going to be Joseph.'

There was a gasp from the class.

'We are not having any shepherds, or any wise men, or an innkeeper, or Herod, or any of those usual things that we have.'

More gasps.

'This year we are going to tell the story from a different point of view. We are going to tell the story from the animals' point of view. All the animals in the story are going to say what they saw and what they thought it meant. We will still sing carols and we will still need a narrator, but other than that, we will all play the parts of different animals in the story.

'Now, who would like to be a camel?'

No one put up their hand.

'Or a sheep?'

Still no movement.

'Or one of the oxen?'

Silence.

'Come on, now,' enthused Mrs Watkins. 'This will be different. This will be a lot of fun. Gary, how about you? I think you would make a terrific camel!'

Gary scowled. 'I could bring in my snake, Miss. Was there a snake in the stable?'

'Don't be so silly, Gary. There was no snake in the Christmas story—and, anyway, I don't think you've got a pet snake, have you, dear? Now then,' she continued, 'do I have any volunteers?'

Eventually, Amanda Goodchild put up her hand.

'Please, Miss. We're going to need a donkey—the donkey that carried Mary. Please, Miss, I would very much like to be the donkey in the play.'

'Ah, Amanda. Of course, you're right. We will need a donkey. But, unfortunately, that part is taken.' And unless Naughty Nora was very much mistaken, she felt sure that at that moment, Mrs Watkins turned very slightly towards her and gave her the briefest of winks.

So the play was arranged. Gary, along with Keenan and Cameron, ended up as a rather fine trio of camels. There were oxen that lived in the stable, and Tabita was a rather grumpy but kind-hearted rooster, who was also the narrator of the story. There were lots of birds who had flown in the sky with the angels and who told that part of the story, and Amanda Goodchild purred with pleasure when she got the part of Mary's cat, who, as it turned out, had been in the room dozing by the fire at the very moment when the angel Gabriel had come to visit Mary to tell her she would be having a baby. And there were lots of sheep out in the field on the night of that baby's birth.

One by one, as the narrator told the whole story, the different animals told what they had seen and heard that wondrous night, and in between the different bits of the story they sang carols. The mums and dads and grandmas and grandads who came to see it said it was the best nativity play they had seen for years. The mums even stopped complaining about the animal costumes they had had to make. (It was so much easier to put a tea towel on your children's heads and turn them into shepherds.)

But who had the starring role in the play? Well, the donkey, of course. The highlight of the story was when the class sang 'Little donkey'. And who played the donkey? Well, you've probably guessed already. It was Naughty Nora, for when Mrs Watkins had asked all the class to write down who they wanted to be, this is what Nora had written:

'I don't want to be Mary or Joseph, and I'd probably never be chosen anyway because I'm too naughty. And I don't want to be a shepherd again, or an angel. I've been a shepherd or an angel for the past six years. And I don't want to be one of the wise men's female assistants. It doesn't say anything about female assistants in the Bible, and if you're not going to have wise women, then I don't want to be one at all. And I certainly don't want to be the innkeeper's wife. She never says anything but just stands next to her husband, nodding her head like an idiot whenever he says there's no room.

'What I'd like to be in the nativity play is the donkey. The donkey is my favourite character, because the donkey did something for Jesus. Everyone wants all the big parts in the play, but it seems to me that Christmas—the real Christmas—is for the little people, not the big ones. The donkey just played a little part, but it was really important. And I know it doesn't mention donkeys in the Bible either, but whenever we think of Mary and Joseph travelling to Bethlehem we think of a donkey.

'I imagine that donkey carrying his precious load, and then I imagine Jesus being laid in a manger—which is actually a feeding trough for the animals—and I think that we should be like the donkey. We should carry Jesus. We should make room for Jesus. We should allow Jesus into our lives like the donkey allowed Jesus into his. Mrs Watkins, if you need a donkey in your play this year, I would like to be it.'

And so she was!

Questions to explore with the children

Have you ever been in a nativity play? Which part did you play? Have you ever wished that you could play one of the main parts? Who do you think are the most important people in the story? Have you ever wondered about the animals in the story and all the amazing things they saw?

 ## Jesus says...

'I am sending you, just as the Father has sent me.'
JOHN 20:21

We are the ones who need to tell people about Jesus today. Although we haven't seen him in the way that people saw him when he lived on earth, we learn about him and we see and hear him in other ways. This is what we must share.

In the Bible, we can read the story of Christmas in Matthew 1:18—2:12 and Luke 2:1–20.

 ## Prayer

Gentle God,
thank you for coming to the world in Jesus.
Help us to learn more about his love for us
and share that love in the world. Amen

 ## Retelling the story

You could use traditional crib figures to begin telling this story in its usual way. Then plastic farmyard animals could be used to tell the new version. You could also prepare a copy of what Naughty Nora wrote and then unfold it and read it out as if it were her actual piece of paper.

Chapter 7

What not to keep in your bed

Naughty Nora has a rather bad habit of keeping things in her bed. Now it is quite normal to keep teddy bears and fluffy rabbits and cuddly toys in bed—all children do this, even big children (though some like to keep it a secret). I even know some grown-ups who still have their teddy with them in bed.

Some children will keep a favourite book under their pillow (and sometimes a torch for reading in the dark when they are supposed to be asleep). Some children will even have one or two toys hidden under the covers. And some children keep a photograph under their pillow of someone they love—their mum or dad who doesn't live with them any more, or a brother or sister who lives away from home, or a best friend or favourite cousin.

All this is quite normal—but Naughty Nora had all sorts of things in her bed. They were the sorts of things that really should be kept in a cupboard. The sorts of things that really should be put in a bin. The sorts of things that, if you leave on their own for too long, go off and start to smell!

Delving under Nora's duvet was a journey into the unknown: you never knew what you were going to find. Half the toy cars in her house were haphazardly parked at the bottom of her bed. Then there were assorted action men and Cindy dolls, tucked up alongside teddy bears, glove puppets, toy animals and a large plastic dinosaur. There were half-built Duplo and Lego buildings by her pillow; there were sweet packets, part of the packaging from a PlayStation game, Thunderbirds 2, 3 and 4, several sticks of chalk, a half-eaten biscuit and a whoopee cushion.

There were dirty socks, dried flowers, conkers, bits of string, and the crust from a sandwich that she hadn't eaten. Neither was it unusual to find Pickles fast asleep in the middle of this mess. It really was the most crowded and most uncomfortable bed you can imagine.

Of course, Nora's mum and dad told her to clear out the mess, and now and again she would half-heartedly put a few things away, but within a few days it was chock-a-block again. On one occasion, Nora's mum found a jam jar with a dead stick insect in it when she was making the bed.

'Oh, I wondered where that had got to,' was all that Naughty Nora had to say.

Eventually her mum and dad told her that she absolutely had to keep her bed more tidy.

'It's unhygienic,' her mum told her. This was after she had discovered a half-eaten bowl of coco-pops (with a spoonful of strawberry jam stirred in—another one of Nora's favourites).

'It's bad enough,' said Nora's mum, 'to have an untidy bedroom, but an untidy, unhygienic, overcrowded bed—this is too much.'

Naughty Nora sulked for a bit. She couldn't really see why it bothered them what she kept in her bed. It didn't keep her awake. They said that she couldn't possibly sleep with all that mess, but Nora rather liked the company of her toys and bits and pieces. Why was it that grown-ups were always so worried about things being clean and tidy? But because her mum and dad looked so cross and serious about it, she did try hard. She didn't want to get into more trouble.

For a few months, things went really well. Each morning,

Nora made sure her bed was empty—well, almost empty, but certainly empty and tidy enough to keep Mum and Dad happy.

Slowly, Mum and Dad forgot about the junk in Nora's bed and started going on at her about other stuff; and, slowly, Naughty Nora started sneaking things back into her bed each night.

Now she had to be careful because she didn't want to get into trouble, but her bed was a good place to keep a few special things. It stopped her brother getting at them. He never went near her bed. 'Don't like the smell,' he said. 'What a cheek!' thought Naughty Nora. But it was good. It meant she could keep a few important and treasured possessions hidden down the side of her bed, under the sheet next to the wall. But one day, Dad found them...

It had been a bit of a difficult day. Naughty Nora had been naughty. She had tried an experiment for breakfast: she had cooked her porridge in the microwave oven. It had all gone well until she forgot about it. The bowl she had been using was a bit small, and the porridge had swelled up. She had put it on for a bit too long and gone to do something else, and it had splashed all over the inside of the oven. Then, instead of cleaning the oven out and telling Dad, she had started all over again.

Although it worked OK, the bits of porridge from the first attempt that were stuck to the inside of the microwave went all crusty. Even this wouldn't have been too bad, except that at lunchtime, when Dad was heating up some soup in the microwave, some of the crusty bits of dried porridge fell off into his soup. He didn't notice until it was too late. He kept on saying, 'This soup is a bit lumpy.' Naughty Nora didn't twig what he was on about until he showed her one of the lumps on the spoon, and she said, 'Oh, that must be from my porridge.'

It might have seemed better to tell a fib—only she had learnt how little fibs have a nasty habit of growing into bigger fibs and getting you into real trouble, so she owned up. How was she to know he didn't like porridge? As she said, 'Oh, that must be from my porridge', Dad started going red in the face and choking, and he got very cross.

He was so cross, he started stomping round the house, looking for other things that Nora might have done wrong. That was why he searched her bed—and down the side of her bed, tucked under the sheet against the wall, he found three things. They were three things that shouldn't really be kept in a bed. Three things that gave the bed a rather funny smell. Three things that made Naughty Nora's dad crosser than ever.

First of all, he found an old piece of crumpled newspaper. It was carefully folded and smelt of vinegar. He unwrapped it. Inside was a large shell. Inside the shell was a big handful of sunflower seeds. He came storming downstairs.

'What are these doing in your bed?' he demanded.

Nora looked crestfallen. These were her treasured possessions. She didn't want anyone to find them.

'Well, come on,' said Dad, looking crosser than ever, his face as red as a beetroot.

'It's my treasure,' said Naughty Nora.

'Your treasure!' snorted Dad. 'Your rubbish, more like. This belongs in the bin, not in the bed.'

He was about to go and throw the things away when something in Nora's voice stopped him. It sounded as if she was going to cry.

'Pleeeease,' cried Nora. 'It is my treasure. My most *special* treasure.'

Dad looked at her. 'What do you mean?' he said.

Naughty Nora carefully took the things from his hands. First of all, she held out the newspaper.

'This is the treasure that reminds me of Grandma and Grandad. Don't you remember when I went to stay with them in Yorkshire? Yorkshire is where you get the best fish and chips in the world. And don't you remember, Grandma and Grandad took me out for the day, and we went to the park, and we came home on the bus and we ate fish and chips. Well, this is the paper the fish and chips were wrapped in, and it reminds me of them and of the lovely day out that I had.'

Then she held out the shell. It was a large, pink, scallop shell.

'And this is from our holiday last summer. Don't you remember how Mum and I used to go out looking for shells when the tide was out, and collect things in my bucket and bring it back to the beach to show you? And how we would lay out all the things we'd found and you would judge which one was the most interesting? Well, Mum found this shell, but she let me say I had found it, and you said it was the winner, the most interesting thing on the beach. This shell reminds me of Mum, and reminds me of how Mum loves me and of that lovely holiday we had.'

Finally, she held out the sunflower seeds.

'Surely you remember these, don't you, Dad? These are from the sunflowers we planted last year. We all planted one and we measured them to see which was the biggest. And yours was the winner, and so we collected the seeds from the winning sunflower to plant some more this year. Well, these are the seeds, Dad. They remind me of you.'

Now it was Dad who was looking crestfallen. In fact, if you looked carefully you could even see a small tear in Dad's eye, because you know, even mums and dads cry sometimes. And now it was Dad's turn to say he was sorry.

'I can see I've been a bit of twit,' he said. 'This isn't junk that belongs in the bin, it's precious treasure. I hadn't realized.'

Naughty Nora and Dad gave each other a hug.

'But,' continued Dad, his voice getting slightly stern again, 'precious treasure doesn't belong in bed, either!'

Then he smiled.

'We need to find a special place to keep it so that it won't come to any harm. Let's see if I can find a box with a lock and key where you can keep your special things.'

And that is exactly what they did.

Questions to explore with children

What is your most precious possession? Do you have things that remind you of the people you love, or lovely places you have been to? I wonder how Naughty Nora felt when she thought her treasure was going to be thrown away?

The really important things in life can't be bought or sold with money. Real treasure is to do with the people and the places that we love, and the happy memories we carry with us.

 ## Jesus says...

'Store up your treasures in heaven.'
MATTHEW 6:20

In fact, knowing God's love is the greatest treasure of all.

In the Bible, there are stories that remind us of what is really important in life, like the story of the woman who anointed Jesus' feet with perfume (Mark 14:3–9).

 ## Prayer

Generous God,
thank you for the precious treasure
of our homes and families,
our school and our friends.
Thank you for all the good times we have had.
Help us to make our hearts a treasure chest
of happy memories and of love. Amen

 ## Retelling the story

This story does need props. You definitely need the newspaper, shell and sunflower seeds (although you can obviously substitute other things). You could also collect all the things that Naughty Nora keeps in her bed and show them as the story is told.

Chapter 8

Naughty Nora gives up nothing for Lent

It was nearly Lent. Lent is the time of the year when we get ready for Easter and give things up so that we can appreciate a bit more how lucky we are to have so many good things.

Sue the priest came into school just before Lent and explained it all. She said that she wanted everyone to think about something they were going to give up. She said that when she came to take the assembly on Ash Wednesday (the first day of Lent) everyone would be given a piece of paper and asked to write down what they were giving up. The papers would be collected together and everyone would pray for strength and perseverance to stick at it. She also said that Lent was a good time for taking something on—praying, or reading the Bible, or being extra helpful.

In class, Mrs Watkins encouraged everyone to think about what this meant for them. They sat on the carpet and talked about what they could give up or take on. Gary Wild said that he was going to give up beetroot for Lent.

'That will be quite some sacrifice, Gary,' said Mrs Watkins. 'We all know how much you like beetroot. We remember that huge one that you brought in for harvest festival.'

'Actually, I don't like beetroot,' said Gary. 'I like growing it, but I don't like eating it.'

'Well, that's not really the point,' said Mrs Watkins. 'The

idea is that we give up something we like, something that we have quite a lot of. Then we could give the money we save to charity and, also, when we start having those things again at Easter we appreciate them even more. It makes us more thankful.'

Junji said he was going to give up practising karate on his sister when she wasn't looking.

'Very good. Most sacrificial,' said Mrs Watkins. 'Perhaps you would like to carry that on after Easter as well.'

Amanda Goodchild said that she was going to give up watching television after school and read a book instead. Mrs Watkins said what a good idea that was.

Naughty Nora couldn't think of anything to give up. Last year she had given up biscuits. The year before, she had given up fizzy drinks. The year before that, she had given up chocolate. 'This year,' she thought, 'I need to take something on. I need to do something that will make the world a better place.' But she couldn't think of anything.

When the morning of the Ash Wednesday assembly arrived, Nora still couldn't think of anything. She thought maybe she would just write 'biscuits' on her piece of paper, but she really wanted to think of something better than that. She was sitting at the breakfast table at home, all on her own. She had eaten her cornflakes, washed down nicely with skimmed milk and peanut butter and a big dollop of strawberry jam. She had had three pieces of toast. Nat was in the sitting room with Mum, being tested for his spellings. Dad had gone to work.

Nora sat on her own, and she thought and thought. 'What could I do to make the world a better place? What could I take on for Lent?' She thought about all the wars in the world. She thought about the people who started wars and about all the bombs and guns in the world. She thought about how greedy

people could be. She thought about how greedy she could
be. She hadn't really needed three bits of toast. One or two
would have been fine. She thought about all the people who
wouldn't have any breakfast that day. She thought about the
people who didn't have any homes to go to. She just sat there
and thought and wondered. What could she give up for Lent?

'I wish the world was a more peaceful place,' she said to
herself. Then, realizing it was nearly time to go to school, she
said a very quick prayer—'Please, God, help us make the
world a better place'—and then she and Nat ran for the bus.
Nora still didn't know what to give up or what to take on for
Lent. But sitting on the bus, staring out of the window and
with her head full of thoughts, she suddenly realized what she
must do. It was the best idea she had had in ages.

The Ash Wednesday assembly began with a song. Sue then
told a story about Jesus going into the desert and not having
anything to eat and being tempted by the devil. It was a good
story. Then everyone was given a piece of paper and asked
to write down what they were doing for Lent. It could be
something they were giving up, or it could be something they
were taking on. Sue said that these were the children's Lent
commitments.

Most people around Nora scribbled away for a few minutes.
It looked as if Amanda Goodchild was writing an essay. Nora
just wrote down one word, and then folded her piece of paper
in half. All the pieces of paper were collected in and Sue said
a prayer, asking that God would help everyone to stick at the
things they had decided to do in Lent.

'Now, then,' she said, 'shall we read out one or two of your commitments? We won't know whose they are, but it will be interesting to find out what different people are doing.'

The first one she pulled out said, 'I'm going to give up sweets.'

'Well done, that person,' said Sue. 'Let's hope you can keep it up.'

The next one said, 'I'm going to read my children's Bible.'

'That's the spirit,' said Sue.

The next one said, 'I'm going to give up being selfish and try to share my toys with my friends.'

'Excellent,' said Sue. 'We are all going to have a really good Lent this year, and we're going to be better people at the end of it.'

But the next piece of paper made Sue's face drop. She picked it out; unfolded it, read it to herself, and for a moment said nothing.

'Oh dear. This person is not planning on a very good Lent.'

She handed the piece of paper to Mrs Starling, the head teacher. Mrs Starling's face looked like thunder.

'I'm very sorry, Sue,' she said. 'I was hoping that all the children would take this seriously, but I'm afraid there are often one or two who spoil things.'

She turned to address the children. 'Now then,' she boomed, 'who wrote this?'

Mrs Starling held up the piece of paper. Right in the middle was written a single word: 'Nothing.'

'Who is giving up nothing for Lent?'

Mrs Starling stared with eagle eyes at all the children. She was searching out the culprit. There was silence. Would anyone own up? Who had done it? Sitting near the back, shrinking into herself, Naughty Nora went bright red. It was her piece of paper.

'Come on,' demanded Mrs Starling. 'Someone wrote this. Who is it?'

Very gingerly, Naughty Nora put up her hand.

'I might have guessed,' said Mrs Starling. 'Why am I not surprised that it is you, Nora Grace? The only person who is going to do nothing in Lent.'

'But that's not what it means,' said Nora. 'I can explain,' she pleaded. 'I didn't mean to be rude, Mrs Starling.'

But there wasn't time for explanations. Mrs Starling marched Nora from the hall and, not for the first time, Nora found herself standing outside the head teacher's office. This time, she knew that she hadn't been naughty. She had been misunderstood. So as she stood there, she couldn't help it—she started to cry. It just wasn't fair.

Sue was leaving the school and, as she went out past the head teacher's office, she saw Nora standing there and went over to have a chat.

'Don't cry,' she said. 'I suppose you were just having a joke, and it was bad luck that I pulled your paper out. But it was a bit silly, wasn't it?'

'No,' said Nora, between her sobs. 'I *am* giving up nothing for Lent, and I'm taking nothing on!'

'What do you mean?' said Sue, kindly.

'I decided this morning that every day—just for a few minutes—I'd do nothing. I would just sit still and think about all the problems of the world, and all the mess the world is in, and I'd say a prayer about it. That's what I've decided to do every day in Lent, so I just wrote down "nothing" on my paper.'

Sue went very quiet.

'Oh dear,' she said for the second time that morning. 'I'd better have a chat with Mrs Starling.'

Sue went into Mrs Starling's office, and a few minutes later they both came out. They both looked forlorn and concerned. They chatted with Nora for a few minutes, then Mrs Starling took Nora back to her class and everything was well again. In fact, Mrs Starling said 'sorry' to Nora, and this was something that had not happened before.

The following week, when Sue came in to do her next assembly, she winked at Nora just before she began.

'Today,' she said, 'we are having quite a special assembly, and we are all going to do something that we don't do enough of in school. I got the idea from Nora last week. We are going to do nothing. We are all going to sit still for two or three minutes. We are not going to say anything, and we are not going to do anything. We are not going to sing songs or say prayers or read anything out. We are just going to be still and quiet and we are going to think about what is happening in the world. We are going to think about the good things in the world, and we are going to think about the problems in the world. Then, at the end of the "doing nothing" time, I'll say a prayer.'

Then an astonishing thing happened. The whole school was quiet. No one said anything. No one did anything. Everyone did nothing for two minutes. It was actually quite nice to be there quietly with your thoughts. And when the two minutes were up, Sue said, 'Please, God, help us make the world a better place.'

It was a good way of keeping Lent.

Questions to explore with children

Have you ever been misunderstood? How does it feel to be told off for something that you haven't done? I wonder how Naughty Nora felt when she got told off when really she hadn't done anything wrong?

Can you sit absolutely still for two minutes? When was the last time you were completely quiet? Think about all the noise that is usually around us. How does it feel to be completely still and quiet?

 # Jesus says...

'When you pray, go into a room alone and close the door. Pray to your Father in private.'
MATTHEW 6:6

I think Jesus means that we shouldn't make a big show of praying. Be still and quiet and think about things, and ask God for help.

In the Bible, Jesus teaches his friends to pray (Luke 11:1–8).

 # Prayer

Loving God,
please listen to us when we pray,
and help us to listen to you.
Help us to find a place of quiet
where we can know that you are our God
and get the help we need
to build a world of peace. Amen

 # Retelling the story

Dramatically unfolding a piece of paper with the word 'nothing' written on it in big letters will help with the telling of this story. You could also have some of the other Lent commitments written out, adding to the drama when you read out Naughty Nora's.

Chapter 9

The true meaning of Easter

Naughty Nora's dad didn't like gardening very much. Instead of cutting the grass every week, he would wait until it had grown too long and would then huff and puff crossly as the lawn mower wheezed and struggled to bring it back under control.

The flower beds were worse. Most of the flowers had been overtaken by weeds, and those that did remain looked rather pathetic. Sometimes, in a fit of enthusiasm, Nora would help her dad hack back some of the undergrowth, but it was short-lived and soon the jungle returned.

In the corner of the garden was a compost heap where grass cuttings and other garden waste, and sometimes potato peelings and carrot tops, were heaped together. The idea was to spread the compost on to the flowerbeds to enrich the soil, but this never quite happened. At the end of one summer, the compost heap was covered with weeds. They had started growing in the spring, and all through the summer they had carried on getting bigger and bigger until you couldn't really call it a compost heap at all.

Nora's mum was really cross about it. 'When are you going to tidy up the garden?' she would complain. 'Especially that compost heap—it's an eyesore.'

At this point, Dad would look up from underneath his newspaper, where he had either been snoozing or reading about the cricket—you could never quite tell.

'Oh, later on,' he would say.

But 'later on' never seemed to come. So, after a day when she had been particularly naughty and got into quite a lot of trouble, Naughty Nora decided that she would tidy up the compost heap herself. 'It couldn't be too difficult,' she thought, 'just a lot of weeds that need digging up and clearing away.'

Nora stuck the garden fork into the ground. The earth was quite hard but it gave way beneath her. She put her foot on the top of the fork, like she had seen her dad do, and pushed it in deeper. Then she lifted up the earth, hoping to dislodge the roots of the weeds. But she was in for a surprise. As she lifted the fork into the air, three or four great big potatoes came into view. She stared at them in astonishment. Where did they come from?

She stuck the fork in again, and uncovered more potatoes. In fact, wherever she dug, and underneath all the weeds, were potatoes—tons of them. She ran excitedly into the house.

'Mum! Dad!' she cried. 'Come and see! Look what's growing on the compost heap!'

Mum and Dad came outside. They were as amazed as Nora. Together, all three of them dug and scrabbled across the compost heap. They filled three buckets with the potatoes they dug up. The potatoes were all different types and varieties and colours.

When they sat back in the kitchen, admiring their amazing crop, Mum explained what had happened: 'It was the potato peelings,' she said. 'All those peelings we put there in the spring—they were covered with grass and other compost, and they've grown.' Mum got an old potato from the fridge and showed Nora the little eyes in them and where the shoots came from and how, even from a peeling, a potato plant could grow.

'So they weren't weeds,' said Nora. 'They were potatoes.'

'Yes,' said Dad, in his serious voice. 'Of course they were. Err... that's why I never dug them up till now. I thought you would both like a surprise.'

Mum and Nora looked at Dad with their eyes wide open.

'Dad, you fibber,' said Nora. 'You were as surprised as we were!'

'Yes, but for once it was a good thing you are so lazy about the gardening,' said Mum. 'Now then, Nora, what would you like for tea? Potatoes?'

All that happened at the end of last summer, but the following Easter Nora had reason to remember it. The school was getting ready for an Easter assembly. Mrs Watkins told everyone to bring something into school that reminded them of the true meaning of Easter. It was to be a surprise and each person was going to come out to the front and show the rest of the class what they had brought.

'Can I bring my snake in?' asked Gary Wild. 'He could represent the devil tempting Jesus.'

'Well, that's an interesting idea, Gary,' said Mrs Watkins, 'but we want it to be a surprise. And anyway, I rather think you're imagining you have a snake. Please don't tell fibs, there's a dear.'

Everyone went home and thought about what they could bring. Naughty Nora wanted to bring something different—something that no one else would think of, that would really make everyone think. She thought of all the obvious things, like an Easter egg or an Easter bunny or an Easter chick. All those things spoke about the new life of Easter, but they all seemed a bit boring to Nora.

Then she thought of slightly more unusual things, like some nails to remember Jesus dying on the cross, or some thorns twisted into a crown. This was a better idea, but she felt sure that some goody-goody like Amanda Goodchild would think of it. No, she wanted something completely original.

Remembering that the soldiers who put Jesus on the cross had given him vinegar to drink, she decided that this was the answer—a bottle of vinegar. No one else would think of that. She went into the kitchen to get one, where her dad was busy making tea—a nice shepherd's pie. As she watched him get the food ready, a different idea came to her in a flash—a brilliant idea. It was the best idea she had had in a long time—something that no one else would ever think of. With a big smile on her face, Nora collected up what she needed to take into school and carefully put it in her bag, ready for the next day.

As the school assembly began, all the children in Naughty Nora's class were standing out at the front. After everyone had sung a song, they began to show what they had brought in. Sure enough, there were lots of eggs, bunnies, chicks and other assorted fluffy creatures. One person had brought a wooden cross and, yes, someone had brought some nails.

Amanda Goodchild had brought a torch. She was looking particularly pleased with herself because no one else had thought of this. 'Easter is like a new light dawning on the world,' she said as she swung the beam of her torch around the room. Everyone was very impressed. Amanda Goodchild was beaming almost as brightly as the torch. So was Mrs

Watkins. Naughty Nora scowled, and Mrs Watkins gave her a hard stare.

Gary Wild had made a whip out of some pieces of rope. He also looked pleased with himself, although this time Mrs Watkins was looking rather nervous. He cracked the whip menacingly. He was less convincing when it came to explaining how it fitted into the Easter story, but Nora remembered that Jesus had been whipped before they hung him on the cross.

Tabita had brought in a beautiful African robe that her grandmother had given her. It was woven in one piece, like the robe that Jesus had worn, which had been taken from him.

Naughty Nora was last in the line. As it got nearer to her turn, she began to wonder whether her idea was quite so good after all. In fact, she began to wish she had brought the bottle of vinegar, because no one else had thought of this. The person next to her was showing yet another fluffy pink monstrosity—a bunny, probably. Nora couldn't see because she was slinking back, trying to get out of view, in the hope that she would be forgotten. But Mrs Watkins saw her.

'Come, now, Nora, what have you got to show us? Don't be shy.'

'Oh, nothing, Mrs Watkins,' said Nora. 'I left mine at home.'

'Don't be so silly, girl; we can all see you've got something behind your back. Come on, let's see it. Another chick, is it? Or an Easter bunny?'

Naughty Nora held out a slightly soggy-looking brown paper bag.

'Oh, it's not as good as everyone else's, Miss. Not worth looking at, really.'

'I'll be the judge of that,' said Mrs Watkins, taking the paper bag from Naughty Nora's hand. 'Now what have we here?'

Mrs Watkins opened the bag and out tumbled a great pile of potato peelings. They fell down her front and on to the floor. Everyone laughed—everyone, that is, except Mrs Watkins.

'What on earth...!' she exclaimed, unable to finish her sentence. 'Whatever were you thinking...?' she began. 'S... S... See me afterwards,' she stuttered, marching Naughty Nora to the door of the hall and standing her outside.

The assembly finished. Everyone said a prayer and the head teacher spoke about Easter, making reference to all the things that had been brought in—that is, all the things except for Naughty Nora's potato peelings.

When all the children were back in their classes, Naughty Nora and Mrs Watkins and the head teacher gathered in the head teacher's study. Nora was staring at her shoes, feeling particularly miserable. How could she have been so stupid as to bring potato peelings into school? Now she was really for it.

But the head teacher, although she was cross, spoke kindly to Nora. 'I think we need an explanation,' she said. For a little while Nora didn't say anything, but then she remembered how telling fibs just gets you into even bigger trouble, so she told the truth. She explained why she had brought the potato peelings into school. She explained what had happened the previous summer, all about the weeds growing on the compost heap in the corner of the garden and how she had gone out one evening to dig them up and, to her amazement, discovered the potatoes growing in the ground.

Then she explained how she had thought of this when Mrs Watkins had asked them to bring in something about the Easter story—because the potato peelings were like Jesus. People had thrown Jesus away. They wanted to get rid of him, so they killed him and buried him and wanted to forget all about him. But they couldn't get rid of him, and they couldn't make him go away. He rose again, and it was a fantastic surprise, just like when she had discovered the potatoes growing in the garden.

As she made this little speech, Nora felt so passionate about what had happened that she couldn't help crying a little bit. At the end of her story, she said she was sorry and that she didn't mean to be stupid. But now it was the head teacher and Mrs Watkins' turn to be quiet. They looked at each other bashfully.

'Oh dear,' said the head teacher. 'I rather think it is us who have been a little stupid.'

'Yes,' said Mrs Watkins, 'and a little hasty.'

'We should have given you time to explain,' said the head teacher.

'We are very sorry,' they both said.

So the next day, the last day of term, when all the school were gathered together before the Easter holidays, instead of the head teacher talking to all the children, it was Naughty Nora herself—the naughtiest girl in all the school, the naughtiest girl the school had ever had—who was invited to come out to the front and address everyone. Nora had with her a great big bag of potato peelings, and she told the story of how things in nature have to die before they can live, and how Jesus died on the cross and then rose again. Everyone cheered.

And because Mum and Dad had to peel a mountain of potatoes so that Nora had enough to take into school, they sat down to a humungous shepherd's pie for the second time that week.

Questions to explore with children

What do you know about the Easter story? Have you ever grown any vegetables? What does it feel like to see something growing in the ground, getting larger and larger and then bearing fruit? I wonder how Naughty Nora felt when she got told off for bringing in the potato peelings? Or how she felt when she had to stand in front of the whole school and tell her story?

Jesus says...

'I tell you for certain that a grain of wheat that falls on the ground will never be more than one grain unless it dies. But if it dies, it will produce lots of wheat.'
JOHN 12:24

All around us in the world we see things dying and rising, falling back and then growing again. In autumn the leaves fall from the trees. In spring they come back again. All this reminds us of Jesus dying and rising.

In the Bible there are lots of stories about how Jesus rising from the dead makes a difference to life. Two friends of Jesus are turned around on the road to Emmaus (Luke 24:13–35), God's Holy Spirit comes to his friends at Pentecost (Acts 2:1–12), and Peter and John heal a crippled man (Acts 3:1–10).

Prayer

Amazing God,
in Jesus you died and rose again.
Help us to be amazed at the wonder of your world
and the love you have for all of us. Amen

Retelling the story

What you need most for this story is a big bag of potato peelings, but it is also helpful to have some of the symbols of Easter that the other children bring in: eggs, Easter bunnies, chicks, a wooden cross, some nails and a torch.

Chapter 10

Naughty Nora's favourite day of the year

Can you guess which day of the year is Naughty Nora's favourite? Well, it's not her birthday, and it's not Christmas. It's not Easter. It's not New Year's Eve, and it's not the first day of the summer holidays.

1 April is Naughty Nora's favourite day—April Fools' day, a day just made for mischievous children like Naughty Nora. Last year she played some great tricks. She got up early and, knowing that Dad always had marmalade on his toast at breakfast, put two or three large spoonfuls of curry powder into the marmalade and mixed it together. You should have seen his face when he ate it! He went bright red and had to drink about a pint of water to cool down.

The year before, she had bought some food colouring and some hair dye and had lots of fun. She got up early and made all the milk in the fridge different colours. Nat had green milk on his cornflakes, Dad had red milk in his tea, and Mum had blue milk on her porridge. With the hair dye she had given Pickles a makeover. His rather dull ginger fur became pink with purple highlights. He looked fantastic—the grooviest cat in town. He hadn't minded. In fact, Nora was sure that he preferred the new look—but Mum and Dad had got rather cross, and she ended up in lots of trouble.

Her most elaborate plan yet had been to steal Dad's car. She had chatted to the man next door, saying that if she took Dad's car keys out of his pocket and popped round early on the morning of April Fools' Day, perhaps he could just go and park it round the corner. It would give Dad a really good fright. For some reason, though, the man next door didn't think it was such a good idea.

Best of all, though, was the year she had found out where the buzzer was, to ring the school bell. It was in the secretary's office, where they usually sent you if you were feeling ill. So she had told her teacher that she was feeling a bit sick and, when she was sitting in the secretary's office, and it was still at least half an hour before playtime, she had rung the bell while the secretary was out of the room. Everyone in the school had extra playtime, Nora included. She had run outside to play, telling her teachers that she was now feeling a lot better and that the fresh air would do her good. She got found out, of course, when the head teacher, Mrs Starling, looked at her watch and wondered why everyone was out at play—but it was worth it.

As 1 April approached, Nora thought and thought about what to do. This year had to be the best ever. She had her reputation to think of. But she just couldn't think of a way of topping all her previous pranks. At last, an idea came to her— a toe-curlingly brilliant idea, an idea that would have Mum and Dad and Mrs Watkins on their guard all day long. This was the trick to end all tricks. On 31 March, Naughty Nora went to bed with a wicked smile on her face.

Can you guess which day of the year is the one that Mum and Dad and Mrs Watkins and Mrs Starling dread the most? Well,

I expect you probably can: it's April Fools' Day. Naughty Nora had caught them so many times in the past that they dreaded this day coming round each year. As each of them went to bed on 31 March, they wondered what on earth would await them in the morning.

Dad got up bright and early. He was relieved to see that Nora was still in bed. But just in case it wasn't actually her under the covers (perhaps she was hiding somewhere in the room, waiting to jump out at him), he gave the bed covers a poke. Nora groaned. It was her all right. He was safe for the time being. But what had she prepared downstairs?

Mum got up. They both trod gingerly around the house.

'What's going on?' said Dad. 'What has she got planned this year?'

'It will happen soon enough,' said Mum, with a sigh.

They opened every door with extra care, wondering whether something was going to topple on to them. They went down the stairs as if they were tiptoeing through a minefield. They entered the kitchen as if they were about to go before a firing squad. At any moment, they were sure, something dreadful was going to happen.

Meanwhile, Naughty Nora got washed and dressed and ready for school. She too came downstairs and watched her anxious parents with an amused look on her face. They started breakfast. Dad seemed to have lost his appetite. He looked at his food suspiciously. He sniffed the marmalade. He held the toast up to the light. He spent ages examining the butter. He sipped his tea as if it might be poison. But it wasn't— everything tasted fine.

Mum was also looking stressed. She stirred her porridge about ten times before eating the first mouthful. She inspected the orange juice and had a good close look at every cup, bowl, plate, knife and spoon before any of them were used. Even when she turned on the tap to begin the washing-up, she did so with extreme caution, as if something were going to come bursting out and attack her. But everything was fine. It was most worrying.

Nora just sat there eating her breakfast. She didn't say anything but she had a huge grin on her face. When Nora went and got her books ready for school, Mum whispered to Dad, 'What's she up to?'

'I don't know,' said Dad. 'But I know it will be something horrible.'

Dad got ready for work. 'Where are my keys?' he wondered. But they were hanging up in their normal place. Where was his jacket? But there it was, hanging on the peg. Where was his wallet? He slowly put his hands into his jacket pocket. Was there going to be something horrible lurking inside? No, everything was quite normal. There was his wallet in its normal place.

He went to put on his shoes. Suddenly he stopped dead in his tracks. His shoes—of course! There would be something horrible in his shoes—toothpaste or tomato ketchup or cold porridge. Why hadn't he thought of this before? He carefully picked them up and cautiously turned them upside down. There was nothing in them. It was all perfectly normal.

'This isn't right,' said Dad. 'Nothing's wrong.' He shook his head in disbelief. It was really very worrying indeed.

Dad went back into the kitchen to say goodbye to Mum, who was now also getting ready to go out to work.

'Watch out for your shoes,' whispered Dad.

'Why, was there something in yours?' asked Mum nervously.

'No,' said Dad, with a look of exasperation on his face. 'They were fine. But you never know. There's got to be something...'.

'Whatever it is, she's got us good and proper this year,' said Mum. 'I just wish she'd get on with it.'

Nora came back into the kitchen.

'Everything all right?' she said in a bright and breezy voice. Mum and Dad stared at her.

'Yes,' they said. 'Everything's fine.'

Dad set off for work, but before getting into his car he walked all round it a couple of times. He even got down on his hands and knees and looked inside the exhaust pipe. Out of the corner of his eye he saw Nora watching him out of the window, peeping from behind the curtains. She was still smirking. 'She's definitely up to something,' he thought. But what was it? He walked round the car again and then got in and drove to work. Nora and Nat then got the bus to school and Mum went to work, and everything was just the same as every other day... except that Mum and Dad were both a bundle of nerves.

At school it was the same. Mrs Watkins came into class looking warily all around her. She opened her desk as carefully as she possibly could. She was convinced that something was going to jump out at her. All through the morning she was looking anxiously about herself. She winced every time she turned her back on the class. Every time Naughty Nora put up her hand, she was sure some dastardly trick was about to be played on her. But everything was normal—too normal, worryingly normal.

When the clock ticked round to twelve o'clock, far from heaving a sigh of relief that the time for tricks was over, Mum and Dad and Mrs Watkins were more sure than ever that something horrendous was about to happen—but nothing did. Other children played tricks on each other, and Nora played a few tricks on her friends. Gary Wild said he wished he'd brought his snake into school—that would have frightened everybody. He could have hidden the snake in someone's gym bag. But people told him to stop telling fibs about this snake of his.

And so the day went by. Nothing happened to Mum and Dad, and nothing happened to Mrs Watkins. By the end of the day, they were all exhausted with worry. It had been the most anxious day they had ever had. Dad went into Nora's room to say goodnight to her. He lay on her bed and stroked her head. She didn't say anything, but she was still smiling—the same smile that she had had on her face all day.

'Is something going to happen now?' thought Dad, looking nervously up at the ceiling. But all was calm and peaceful.

'Why didn't you play a trick on us today?' said Dad after a while. 'I thought today was your favourite day of the year. I felt sure that something was going to happen. I've been on tenterhooks all day long.'

'But I *did* play a trick,' said Nora. 'Today *is* my favourite day of the year. Something *has* happened. It has been the *best* trick of all.'

'What?' said Dad, still unsure what was happening.

'Not playing a trick was the trick! You should have seen your face! You and Mum and Mrs Watkins—worried all day long that something was about to happen. It was one long trick. April Fools!'

Questions to explore with children

Have you played any really good April Fools? I wonder how Nora's mum and dad felt, waiting for something to happen?

Do you remember a time when you were really surprised by something unexpected that happened? Have you ever been surprised by God? Has something happened that you can't really explain?

 ## Jesus says...

'*No one knows about that day or hour, not even the angels in heaven.*'

MARK 13:32 (NIV)

Life is full of surprises. Unexpected things do happen.

In the Bible we can read about the biggest surprise of all—Jesus rising from the dead. This wasn't what Jesus' friends were expecting. Mary Magdalene meets him in the garden (John 20:11–18), and Paul meets him on the road to Damascus (Acts 22:4–16). We can meet Jesus today. Are we ready to be surprised by him when we see him in other people?

 ## Prayer

Surprising God,
keep us on our toes,
watching and waiting for you
and ready to greet you when you come. Amen

 ## Retelling the story

You may not be able to dye a cat pink, but you could bring in some milk dyed different colours to help with this story. You can also act out different bits, such as looking into shoes or delving into pockets, fearing that something horrible awaits.

Chapter 11

Naughty Nora is transformed

It all started innocently enough. One Monday morning, Naughty Nora came down to breakfast and announced to everyone that she didn't like her hair. She said that she'd been looking at herself in the mirror for a long time and had decided her hair was simply awful.

'It's too long,' she said, 'and it's the wrong colour. I wish I had red hair, or blonde hair. I wish my hair was curly. My hair is boring.'

'Don't be so silly,' said Dad. 'Your hair is lovely.'

But things only got worse. On Tuesday, Nora came down and said that she wished she was taller.

'I'm too small,' she said. 'I'm not elegant enough.'

On Wednesday, she said that she thought her eyes were the wrong colour. Her eyes were brown, but blue eyes were definitely better. On Thursday, she said that she wished she was left-handed.

'It's very boring being right-handed,' she said. 'Nearly everyone is right-handed. I want to be left-handed. It isn't fair!'

When Nora came down on Friday, everyone was dreading what she would say next, but instead she was sullen and silent and didn't say a word.

'Everything all right this morning?' said Dad after a while.

'Actually, no,' said Nora, defiantly. 'My nose is too small. I hate my nose. If you want to buy me something for my birthday this year, you can get me plastic surgery.'

With that, she stormed out of the room. Nat sniggered.

'We could always get a large paper bag to put over her head,' he suggested. 'That would solve most of the problems.'

'I heard that!' screamed Nora from the hall. Then a big fight began, and that evening Mum and Dad sat up talking about Nora, wondering what on earth she was going to say next and worrying about why she felt so unhappy about how she looked.

'Perhaps it's all those magazines,' said Mum, 'with pictures of super-thin models, looking impossibly perfect. Nora doesn't look like them, thank goodness. They look like they could do with a good meal. Nora looks lovely as she is, but she just doesn't realize it. I'll tell her tomorrow how good she looks.'

But on Saturday morning—a day when you don't have to get up early and put on school uniform—things were worse than ever. Naughty Nora got up at about nine. She spent ages in the shower. She then spent ages in her bedroom. She then went back to the bathroom, locked the door and was in there for another half an hour.

When she eventually came downstairs, it was the middle of the morning, and she looked extraordinary. She was wearing a pair of high-heeled shoes that she'd borrowed from Mum. They were four sizes too big. Her hair was sort of in curls—she had done something with Mum's curling tongs. She was wearing her old bridesmaid's dress, but the wedding had been two years ago, and the dress was now too small for her. Her face was plastered with make-up: thick black eyeliner, mascara, foundation, blusher and bright red lipstick. For someone who was usually such a tomboy, it was quite a transformation. Although Mum was shocked, she decided not to say anything.

'Oh, you look nice,' she said, trying to sound as if she

didn't have a care in the world and it was perfectly normal for Nora to dress this way.

'This is the new me,' said Nora.

'Can I get you anything for breakfast?' said Mum.

'Oh, half a grapefruit. That will be all.'

In the afternoon, Nora asked if they could go shopping. She wanted to buy some hair dye, some make-up of her own, and some high-heeled shoes that fitted. Mum said, 'Hasn't all this gone a bit far?' and they ended up having an argument. It was all getting very difficult—but Dad had a plan. That evening, when Nora and Nat were in bed, Dad spent ages in the kitchen fiddling around with something. Mum didn't know what he was up to. When he had finished, he had a big smile on his face.

The next morning was Sunday. Nat was having his breakfast in front of the telly. Mum was getting changed, ready to go to church. It was just Dad and Nora at the breakfast table.

'Can I get you anything?' said Dad.

'Perhaps I'll have an apple,' said Nora.

'Help yourself,' said Dad. 'I, on the other hand, am really hungry. I want a plate of something filling.'

He went to the cupboard and started rummaging around. To Naughty Nora's horror and surprise, he came back to the breakfast table with a big packet of cat food. He opened it up and poured a huge helping into his bowl. He then poured some milk over the top and started gobbling it down just as if it were a normal bowl of cereal.

'Dad, have you gone mad?' said Nora.

'Oh, it's delicious,' said Dad, between mouthfuls. 'You really ought to try it.'

'But it's cat food!'

'Yes, and jolly tasty cat food it is, too.'

'But, Dad, it can't be good for you. It's not meant for humans.'

'Don't be so silly,' said Dad. 'Try a mouthful.'

He held out a spoonful to Nora, but she grimaced and said she was going to get Mum. When Mum came into the kitchen, she was as surprised as Nora, but all Dad could say was, 'Go on, try a mouthful. It's delicious. Where is your sense of adventure? Don't you think you need to open your mind to new experiences?'

Nora examined the bowl of cat food. It looked OK. Usually she was the first person to try something crazy like this. Nobody ate stranger combinations of food than she did. She decided to give it a go.

'Come on, then,' she said, and helped herself to a spoonful of the cat food. She sniffed at it tentatively. It smelt all right. She put the tiniest little amount on the end of her tongue. It tasted all right. With a gulp, she put the spoon into her mouth. Dad was right, it tasted good. But Mum was looking furious.

'What is going on?' she cried. 'Has the whole world gone mad? As if we haven't had enough problems this week with Nora deciding she doesn't like the way she looks, now I've got the two of you eating cat food for breakfast!'

Dad smiled broadly. 'Don't worry,' he said, 'it's not cat food.'

He then explained to them what he had done the night before. He had found a new packet of cat food and very carefully opened it at the bottom of the packet. He had taken out the cat food and replaced it with a mixture of All Bran and sunflower seeds.

'You thought it was cat food,' he said to Nora, 'because you could see the packet. It said "cat food" so you thought it must be cat food. But it isn't. You see, you can't always judge things by what's on the outside.'

He then leaned over and held her hands tightly.

'You're worried about what you look like on the outside—your hair, your eyes, your size, your clothes—and it is normal to worry about these things. Most people do at one time or another. But what matters is what's on the inside. That is the real person. I think you look great on the outside, and so do most people, but I'm absolutely sure that you are even more beautiful on the inside. That's what's really important.'

'Even though I can be such a twit?' said Nora, suddenly realizing what Dad was saying to her and why he had played his trick with the cat food.

'That's you. And we like you just the way you are—inside and out!'

'And we'll like you even better if you hurry up and get your coat and shoes on, so that we can get to church,' said Mum, looking at the clock.

There was a flurry of activity, and they all got out of the door in time. At church that morning, the reading said not to worry about what you eat and what you wear. The birds have food to eat and the flowers all look beautiful, and God loves and cares for you even more than he cares for them. This made Naughty Nora think. Dad was right. It wasn't her outward appearance that mattered and, anyway, God thought she was beautiful whatever she looked like. It was the inside that was important.

As they were walking home, Nora told Dad that she had decided perhaps it was OK to have black hair and brown eyes and to be right-handed, after all.

'I'm very pleased to hear it,' said Dad. 'The cat food did the trick.'

'And the reading this morning made me think.'

'That's good. You know, there's another bit in the Bible where Jesus says that every hair on your head is counted, whatever the colour! Isn't that amazing?'

Nora looked up at her dad's balding head.

'Not so difficult in your case!' she said.

Questions to explore with children

I wonder why Naughty Nora felt so unhappy about how she looked? Have you ever felt like this?

Has anyone ever made fun of you because you weren't wearing the right clothes? What do you think is really important—what someone is like on the outside or what they are like on the inside?

Jesus says...

'I tell you not to worry about your life. Don't worry about having something to eat, drink, or wear. Isn't life more than food or clothing? Look at the birds in the sky! They don't plant or harvest. They don't even store grain in barns. Yet your Father in heaven takes care of them. Aren't you worth more than birds? Can worry make you live longer? Why worry about clothes? Look how the wild flowers grow. They don't work hard to make their clothes. But I tell you that Solomon with all his wealth wasn't as well clothed as one of them.'

MATTHEW 6:25–29

Jesus teaches us that God loves us whoever we are and whatever we look like. God cares for us all. God is concerned about the inside of a person, not the outside. We should be the same.

In the Bible, it says that everyone is made in the image of God. We find this in the story of how God made the very first man and woman (Genesis 1:26–31).

Prayer

Loving God,
you love us inside and out.
Help us to love ourselves and to love each other,
regardless of what we look like.

Help us never to judge someone by the colour of their skin,
or by their clothes,
or by the way they talk.
Give us eyes to see people on the inside
and to love them with the same love you show us in Jesus. Amen

Retelling the story

This story really works well if you act out the eating of the cat food, without telling the children what is happening.. This requires a bit of preparation, but it is not difficult to replace the cat food with a mixture of bran and seeds. Carefully open the box at the bottom and then, when you have made the switch, glue it back together.

At the point in the story where Dad eats the cat food, you need to eat it yourself. The children will groan with horror, but it works really well and helps to emphasize the point about not judging things by what you see on the outside.

Chapter 12

Water, water

Did you know that every time you run a bath, you use 80 litres of water? And did you know that every time you have a shower, you use 35 litres—and every time you flush the toilet, you use 10 litres? Every person in Britain uses about 135 litres of water—that is 238 pints—every day, yet a quarter of all the people in the world don't even have safe drinking water, let alone baths or showers or toilets. Hundreds of children die every day because they don't have clean water. We take water for granted. We just turn on the tap and it's there. But what if it wasn't? What if we suddenly found we had to treat water with a bit more care?

It was a hot day—a very hot day—the hottest day of the year so far. Naughty Nora had hardly slept. All through the night she had tossed and turned in her bed, throwing the duvet on to the floor and hoping it might cool down, or even that it would rain. But the morning, when it came, seemed hotter than ever.

Nora padded her way into the bathroom, wiping the sleep from her eyes. She cleaned her teeth. She washed her face and, leaving the cold tap running, she put her hands under the steady stream of cool water. It was a delicious feeling, but it didn't stop her feeling hot and bothered. She turned on the shower and, making sure the knob was turned right round on to the coldest setting, she put her head under the flow of water. It felt really good. She stood there for several minutes and at last felt herself cooling down. She shook her hair dry and went downstairs for some breakfast. Upstairs in the bathroom, the cold tap was still running. So was the shower. She had left them both on.

It was a Saturday morning and Mum and Dad and Nat had already eaten breakfast. Nora didn't feel particularly hungry, so she went outside into the blazing heat of the summer morning. The sun was still quite low in the sky, but it was already getting very hot. It was so hot that she imagined that the tarmac in the road would soon be sticky underfoot.

Somewhere Nora had read that on a very hot day you could fry eggs on the bonnet of a car. Today seemed like the perfect day to try out such an experiment. Mum was sitting in the back garden, reading the newspaper. Dad was tidying up in the lounge. Naughty Nora took a box of eggs from the fridge and went out on to the front drive.

One by one she broke the eggs on to the bonnet of Dad's car. They didn't so much sizzle as run, trickling down the front of the car on to the headlights. She was on to her third egg, and just wondering whether she should have waited till later in the day when the car would have soaked up a bit more of the sun, when Dad came out and yanked the eggbox out of her hands.

'What on earth are you playing at?' he exclaimed. He was so cross that he pulled on the eggbox a little too hard. One of the eggs flew out and broke down his front. The egg ran all over his shirt and tie. He looked at Nora crossly. 'You naughty girl!' he said. 'What do you think you're doing? Making breakfast?'

'Well, yes, actually,' replied Nora. 'I was seeing if you really could fry eggs on the bonnet of a car. It said in the newspaper that you could.'

'Well, you can't,' said Dad. 'At least, not on my car. Now clear up this mess, and I'll go and change.'

Nora went and filled a bucket of water from the tap on the wall at the side of the house. She was feeling hot again. Before filling up the bucket, she placed her hands under the flow of the water. It felt lovely. It was also nice to see the water running down the path and into the drain. She filled up the bucket and, leaving the tap running, went round the front of the house to clean the car. When she had finished, she went inside. Dad had changed his shirt and had calmed down a bit.

'I'm sorry,' she said. 'It was just an experiment.'

Dad made a sort of harrumphing noise and went back to his tidying and cleaning. Mum came in from the garden. She had heard what had happened and thought it was rather funny. She wished she had seen Dad with the egg all down his shirt, but she wisely decided it was best not to say so. She winked at Nora as he left the room.

'Perhaps we'll try later, when it's got really hot,' she said. 'Now why don't you get yourself back in Dad's good books by washing up those breakfast things?'

Naughty Nora set to work. It was too hot to use the hot water. Instead, she ran the cold tap and held the dirty bowls and plates under the jet of water. It sprayed a bit, but that didn't matter. It cooled her down. Soon the washing-up was done. Nora left the kitchen with yet another tap running.

Mum and Dad and Nat were now all in the back garden. Nat was playing with his cars. Mum and Dad were reading the paper and arguing over who should have which bits. Nora didn't know what to do. She kicked a football around for a few minutes, but it was too hot for that. She played catch with herself. She thought about getting out her skipping rope, but it was definitely too hot for skipping.

She wandered round the edge of the garden, absent-mindedly trailing her hand through the shrubs and flowers. She pulled at the big red flowers on the rose bush and let the petals fall to the ground. She scrabbled in the earth, picking them up again, and played on the grass, making the petals into different patterns. She then collected sticks and stones from the flowerbeds and made even more intricate patterns and designs. The morning whiled away. Nat was still playing. Dad was snoring. Mum was puzzling over the crossword.

'Anyone fancy a cup of tea?' said Nora.

'Oh, yes, please,' said Mum. 'Put the kettle on and I'll come in in a minute and give you a hand.'

Then she whispered, 'Dad's asleep at the moment so we might try frying another egg.'

Mum looked at Nora's hands. They were covered in dirt. 'Before you do anything else, my girl, you need to give those hands a wash.'

Nora went into the downstairs bathroom. She put on the cold tap and again let her hands bathe in the flow of the water. It felt so nice that she just stood there for several minutes with the water gushing out.

Upstairs in the bathroom, the cold tap was running. So was the shower. The tap by the side of the house was running. So was the tap in the kitchen. Now the tap in the downstairs bathroom was running as well. Nora had turned on every tap in the house and every tap in the house was gushing out water!

Mum came indoors. She was followed by Dad, who had woken up from his snooze and was going to use the bathroom upstairs.

'What are you doing, Nora?' Mum shouted. 'Have you put that kettle on yet?'

She saw Nora running her hands through the water.

'Don't leave the water on like that,' she said. 'It's a waste.'

Mum went into the kitchen. At that very moment Dad went into the bathroom. And at the same moment Nat rolled one of his cars round to the side of the house. Each of them saw the taps running and they all converged in the hallway.

'Who left the tap and the shower running upstairs?' said Dad.

'Who left the tap running in the kitchen?' said Mum.

'Who left the tap running outside?' said Nat.

They all looked at each other. They all shrugged their shoulders as if to say 'It wasn't me.' They all looked towards the downstairs bathroom. They could hear another tap running. Dad pulled open the door, and there was Naughty Nora running her hands under the water.

'Nora, have you left the taps running upstairs?' said Dad.

'And in the kitchen?' said Mum.

'And outside?' said Nat.

Nora's face fell. 'Oh lummy,' she said.

'Don't you know there's a water shortage?' said Dad.

'Don't you know it's a waste?' said Mum.

'Don't you know there are millions of people who don't have any water at all?' said Nat. 'To stay alive, a person needs two and a half litres of water a day. You've just wasted enough water for hundreds of people! Don't you know that every eight seconds a child dies because they don't have fresh water?'

Mum and Dad looked at Nat with amazement. They didn't know he knew these things.

'We did it at school,' he said, smiling.

'Oh dear,' said Nora. 'I am sorry. I wasn't thinking.'

Dad decided that Naughty Nora needed to be taught a lesson. He didn't say anything straightaway—except for telling her to be more careful—but a plan was forming in his mind.

That night, when Nora was fast asleep in bed, Dad turned the stopcock under the sink in the kitchen and shut off the supply of water to the house. Now it was impossible to get any water. He told Mum and Nat what he was doing, but he didn't tell Nora.

The next day was as hot as ever. Nora got up and went into the bathroom. She turned on the tap to clean her teeth, but nothing came out. 'That's funny,' she thought, and tried the shower. But no water came out of there either. She went downstairs, but it was the same with the taps in the kitchen and the bathroom. No water came out at all. Dad was sitting at the kitchen table, eating a piece of toast.

'Dad!' said Nora. 'There's no water!'

'Yes, I noticed,' said Dad calmly. 'You must have used up our supply yesterday. They only give a certain amount to each house at the moment.'

'But, Dad, we can't survive without water. What will we wash with? How will we clean our teeth? How will we make a cup of tea?'

'Oh, I managed to drain off a little bit of water when I got up earlier. It's in a jug in the fridge. There will be enough for everyone to have a glass of water, and maybe just a little to clean teeth and wash hands, but that will be it for today.'

'But I was planning to have a shower this morning!'

'Well, that will have to wait till tomorrow... or maybe the next day.'

'Tomorrow!' exclaimed Nora. 'The next day! This is an outrage. How can they do this?'

'Well, Nora,' said Dad, 'it was you who left the taps on.'

So all that day there was only the smallest amount of water, and all that day Nora felt miserable about what she had done. She promised herself that she wouldn't leave taps running again, and also promised herself that she would treat water with much more respect.

In the evening, Dad went on the computer and showed Nora a website about water conservation and about how many people in the world manage on very little water at all—about the same as they had had that day. He then took her into the kitchen, showed her the stopcock under the sink and explained what he had done.

At first Nora was cross, but then, as Dad smiled at her and gave her a hug, she realized she had learnt an important lesson. She wouldn't be wasting water again, and by saving water she might be doing just a little bit to help people in other parts of the world. For just one day, she had been given a little taster of what life was like for them.

Questions to explore with children

Think of how many times we use water every day: I wonder what it would be like to manage with only a tiny amount? How would it feel to turn on the tap and find that nothing comes out?

 ## Jesus says...

'*When I was thirsty, you gave me something to drink.*'
MATTHEW 25:35

When we share what we have with people in need, it is as if we are sharing it with Jesus himself.

In the Bible there are stories about sharing. Jesus goes to a wedding and the wine runs out. He turns water into wine and shares it with everyone (John 2:1–11).

 ## Prayer

Generous God,
you have given us a wonderful world,
with water and food and flowers and trees—enough for everybody.
Help us not to be so greedy
and not to take your world for granted,
and not to abuse and spoil your world.
As we learn to share things with others,
help us to see we are sharing them with you. Amen

 ## Retelling the story

Nat gives a statistic for how much water many people have to live on. Measuring out this amount of water and showing the children how little it is makes for a dramatic way of underlining the message of this story—which, of course, has other ecological implications that can be brought out, concerning how we must learn to conserve and respect the earth.

Chapter 13

What to do on a rainy day

After the sun came the rain. Dad said to Nora that he knew it was going to rain because they were going on holiday the next day. In fact, he said, he had thought about phoning up the weather people to tell them the Grace family were going on holiday so they may as well cancel whatever other predictions they were going to make. It was bound to rain.

And rain it did—hour after hour, and day after day. Sometimes there would be a brief break in the clouds and the sun would peep through. Mum, Dad, Nora and Nat would all crawl out of the tent and try to look cheerful, and then the skies would open again. Everyone was very miserable. Four people together in a leaky tent for a rainy week is not an easy thing to enjoy.

Dad kept on trying to cheer everyone up by suggesting another game of I-spy or cards or travel Scrabble, or another dash to the shop on the campsite, or trips in the car to the cinema in the nearby town. But they had seen the only film that was on, and it wasn't worth seeing twice.

'I'm bored,' said Nora on day three of their wet holiday.

'I'm *very* bored,' said her brother.

'I'm fed up with the rain,' said Nora.

'I'm *very* fed up with the rain,' said Nat.

Dad had an idea. 'Let's go to the beach,' he said.

'But it's raining!' complained Nora and Nat.

'But that means it will be easy to park,' replied Dad

cheerfully. 'And we won't have any trouble finding a space on the beach.'

'But what will we do?'

'Pack the umbrellas,' said Dad, 'and I'll show you.'

Mum stayed behind to read her book and Nora and Nat reluctantly filed into the car behind Dad. It was a short drive to the beach and, as expected, the car park was virtually empty. So was the beach. It was only drizzling now, but the beach was still a miserable place to be on a wet day. Dad marched Nora and Nat over to a café. He bought them each a comic and a bag of chips and gave them money to buy an ice cream afterwards.

'I'll be back in half an hour,' he said. 'Wait here, and behave yourselves!'

He had a quick chat with the woman behind the counter, who told him that she would keep an eye on the two children, and off he went. Nora and Nat looked at each other. What on earth was going on?

'If it wasn't raining so much,' said Naughty Nora, 'I'd say Dad has had too much sun.'

Half an hour later, Dad returned. He had a big grin on his face.

'Right, then,' he said. 'Time for a treasure hunt. Now it's my turn to sit in the café and yours to find the buried treasure.'

He handed the children a piece of paper. On it were written these strange words:

> Start with what goes inside computers
> and nicely with fish.

'What does this mean?' said Nora.

'That's what you must find out,' said Dad.

The two children stood outside the café, staring at the piece of paper. It seemed to be gobbledygook.

'Start with what goes inside computers and nicely with fish...' said Nora.

Suddenly she perked up. 'Chips!' she said.

'What?' retorted Nat.

'Chips,' said Nora. 'Chips is what you get inside computers and what goes nicely with fish. It's chips.'

'But what could it mean?' thought the children, looking around hopefully. They were standing outside the café. In front of them was a great big sign, and in great big letters it said, 'Fish 'n' chips'. They looked at it together and the same thought came into their heads. Blu-tacked to the back of the sign, behind where it said 'chips', was an envelope. They fought over the envelope and nearly tore it in half, but eventually opened it. Inside was a piece of paper that read:

> **Go one hundred paces left, take off one and what have you got?**

By now, the two children were facing each other. 'This way,' they both said, pointing in opposite directions and beginning to head off away from each other.

'This can't be right,' said Nora. 'Which way do we go?'

'This way,' said Nat crossly.

'No, this way,' said Nora.

The two children stood arguing for a few minutes. Both insisted that their way was right, but neither of them really knew. It was one of those silly arguments that people often have. Nat started walking off in his direction, muttering under his breath that Nora never let him get his way. Nora followed, also muttering angrily.

Nat was counting the steps out loud, but when he got to 67, he found himself standing up against the cliff that bordered the beach. At this point, Nora could have been nice and explained gently that it must be her way, but instead she declared triumphantly, 'There, I told you it was my way. I knew I was right!' Actually, she didn't know she was right—she had just been lucky—but she wasn't prepared to admit that to Nat.

She headed back to the café, with Nat trailing behind her, and started counting out a hundred steps. When she got to a hundred, she found herself standing outside an ice cream stall, all on its own at the edge of the beach.

'Now take one off,' said Nat. 'You've forgotten that bit. It said, "Go one hundred paces left, take off one and what have you got?"'

The children took a step backwards. They were still outside the ice cream stall.

'Now what?' said Nora.

'Perhaps it was my way after all,' said Nat. 'Perhaps we should have taken smaller steps.'

They were just about to start arguing again when Nora suddenly realized what it meant.

'Ninety-nine!' she exclaimed.

'What?'

'Ninety-nine! The ice cream. Ninety-nine! Look, there's a sign. I'm so clever!' said Naughty Nora, proudly. 'I've got the clue. I'm so clever, and you're so stupid.'

Nat frowned and made a face at Nora. Sure enough, behind the ice cream sign was another envelope and another clue.

Nora read it out:

> **Even King Canute can't save this castle.**

'What on earth does that mean?' she said. 'Who's King Canute when he's at home?'

But as Nora stood there wondering what it meant, Nat started stomping down to the sea. Nora thought it was because he was cross at being so stupid, but actually it was because he had guessed what the last clue meant and he wasn't going to tell his big sister.

Nat knew about King Canute. King Canute was the crazy old king who had ordered the tide not to come in. So the last clue must be buried by the sea under a castle.

Nat arrived at the water's edge. The tide was coming in but, because no one else was on the beach, there was only one sandcastle to be seen. This had to be the one that Dad had built, and under it would be the next clue.

While Nat scrabbled in the sand, Nora was still up on the promenade, feeling pleased with herself and trying to remember who King Canute was. She saw Nat playing in the sand at the water's edge. 'Silly boy,' she thought.

After a few minutes digging, Nat found the envelope. He opened it up. This time it wasn't a clue, but a map. It seemed to be a map of the beach, and in the centre of the map was a large X. 'The treasure is hidden here,' it said.

'Right,' said Nat, 'I'm going to find this treasure without Nora.' And he started running off towards where he thought the X was marked.

At that moment, Nora suddenly remembered who King Canute was and understood the clue. With horror, she also realized that Nat had got there before her. She looked up and saw him running away from the water's edge. 'He must have the clue,' she thought.

Naughty Nora charged after her brother. He was a fast runner, but she was two years older and soon caught him. She jumped at his legs and pulled him to the ground. She grabbed his arm and tugged the paper from his hands. The map tore in two.

'You idiot!' he cried out, and kicked Nora in the stomach. She wheezed in pain, let go her grip, and a gust of wind caught hold of the paper and blew it high into the air. Nat got up to chase it, tripped, and in the next moment his piece of paper was wafting away as well.

The two children sat, panting on the beach, staring at each other crossly, muttering unprintable words and each blaming the other.

'You ran off without me,' said Nora. 'You're a cheat!'

'You were making fun of me,' said Nat. 'You're selfish!'

And so it went on. They shouted at each other for about five minutes. Then the shouting was about to turn into another fight. Nat went to hit Nora, and Nora went to hit Nat... but then they stopped...

The map was gone. It had started to rain again. They were both fed up with each other and, if they were honest, fed up with themselves.

'I'm sorry,' said Nora. 'I shouldn't have teased you.'

'I'm sorry,' said Nat. 'I shouldn't have run off.'

'Let's look for the clue,' said Nora.

'It wasn't a clue, it was a map,' said Nat.

They got up and started searching the beach. After about five minutes, they found the two torn pieces of map. The paper was rather soggy and all the ink had run. Nora and Nat put the pieces together and could just about make out where the cross was marked. It was leading them back towards the café they had come from, and towards a small boat that was stranded on the beach above the tide line.

'That's where the treasure must be!' said Nat.

They ran up the beach, dived under the boat and there, safely hidden, was another envelope. Their eager hands tore it open. Inside was a £20 note. They both grabbed it at once. They both struggled to have it. They pulled it this way and that... and it tore in half. For a moment, they knelt there staring angrily at each other yet again. Then they burst out laughing.

'Quickly,' said Nora. 'I know what to do.'

They nipped into the café where Dad was sitting reading the paper.

'Finished at last,' he said. 'You took your time.'

But they ignored Dad and went straight up to the woman behind the counter.

'Could we borrow some sticky tape?' asked Nora.

'Why, yes,' said the woman.

She handed Nora the tape. Nora quickly stuck the two halves of the £20 note back together. Smiling, they turned to Dad.

'Did you find the treasure?' he asked.

'Yes,' they replied. 'We're going to share it!'

Questions to explore with children

Have you ever fought with someone over something? I wonder how Naughty Nora and Nat felt when the map tore in two, and then the £20 note?

Sometimes it is hard to share, especially when someone is teasing you or getting cross with you. Have you ever been in a situation when it was hard to share?

 ## Jesus says...

'Treat others as you want them to treat you.'
MATTHEW 7:12

These words of Jesus are sometimes called the Golden Rule. They mean that if you would like people to share with you, then it is best if you share with them. It's a good way of living! It would make the world a better place.

Jesus also told a story about two houses, one built on rock and one on sand (Matthew 7:24–27). He asks us to think about what we are building our life on.

 ## Prayer

Long-suffering God,
when we get angry and impatient with each other,
and when we fail to share,
help us to act with kindness and generosity
so that we can live our lives in the way you want us to. Amen

 ## Retelling the story

Write out the clues on pieces of paper and seal them in envelopes. Then open them at the different points of the story, and invite the children to see if they can solve the clues. It is also very dramatic to tear the map and the £20 note in half to show what happens if we don't share with each other.

Chapter 14

Nora's ark

Nora loved animals. She loved Pickles, the family cat. She loved the dog that lived next door. She loved the birds in the garden and, in the winter, she always made sure they had enough food. And even though Pickles did her best to chase them away, because there was always food there were always birds. She loved the parrot that lived in the house at the end of the street; and she loved it when the woman who also lived there invited her in for a drink and biscuit. The parrot would chatter away, telling everyone what a pretty boy he was.

Therefore, on Nora's birthday, when her parents bought her a hamster, it was the best present she had ever had. She loved that hamster more than anything, and she called him Rooney, after her favourite footballer. When she got up in the morning, she would play with Rooney and make sure his cage was clean and that he had enough to eat. In the evening she would play with him again. She let him run around inside her jumper, and he especially liked crawling up her sleeves. She loved the ticklish feeling it gave her.

But because it is Naughty Nora we are talking about, she also loved getting into mischief with Rooney—slipping him up the sleeve of Mum's jumper, or hiding him inside the cereal packet so that, when Nat poured out his cornflakes, Rooney came tumbling into the bowl.

One day, when the mood for mischief was rising up inside her as it so often did, Naughty Nora decided to smuggle

Rooney in to school. 'There's a lot of fun to be had with a hamster at school,' she thought to herself. So, while she and Nat travelled to school on the bus, Rooney was snuggled down at the bottom of her bag, munching on some seeds that Nora had put there.

When lessons began and Mrs Watkins was reading out the register, Rooney was in Nora's pocket. When Mrs Watkins wasn't looking, Nora was showing him to all her friends. His little head poked out from the top of her pocket and his whiskers twitched. Everyone thought it was great. There was lots of laughing and talking in the classroom. Mrs Watkins sensed that something was wrong, but she didn't know what. 'Nora must be up to something,' she thought.

At playtime, Nora and Amanda Goodchild played with Rooney in the sandpit. Amanda also loved animals and she had always wanted a hamster, so she loved playing with Rooney and stroking his smooth fur. Gary Wild came over to them. 'Snakes eat hamsters,' he said nonchalantly. 'I bet my snake could eat your hamster in one mouthful.' Nora told him to go away and mind his own business and he went off in a huff. 'You haven't got a snake,' she said to him crossly.

In the lessons that followed, Rooney was passed around the class under the table. Most of the children got to stroke him, and Mrs Watkins, though still a bit suspicious, never found out what was going on.

At lunchtime, Nora shared her sandwiches with Rooney. He was now feeling very tired (hamsters usually sleep during the day) so after lunch, while Nora and the rest of the class were painting, Rooney was fast asleep in Nora's bag—or so she thought...

While everyone else was painting, Gary Wild came over to Nora's bag, loosened the buckle and poked Rooney with the end of his paintbrush. Rooney woke in fright, jumped out of the bag and scurried around the classroom, looking for a safe place to go to sleep.

Near the front of the class was a nice big bag. Inside the bag there was a nice woollen hat and scarf. That looked ideal—warm and comfy. Rooney snuggled down inside and went back to sleep.

The school day ended. Mrs Watkins told all the children to put away their things and get their bags ready to go home. While they were doing this, Mrs Watkins got her own bag and put it on her desk with a thump. It was quite a big thump. In fact, it was a big enough thump that, were there to be a hamster curled up asleep inside the bag, it would probably be woken up.

All the children stood by their desks. The bell was about to go. Mrs Watkins reached inside her bag to get her hat and scarf and, at the same moment, Rooney peeked his nose out from underneath Mrs Watkins' hat, his whiskers twitching.

Mrs Watkins screamed. She jumped up on to her chair. As she did this, she knocked her bag on to the ground. Rooney scampered out and ran around her chair. She screamed again. She could hardly get the words out, she was so frightened, but it seemed as if she was saying, 'A rat! A rat! Help! Get the caretaker, there's a rat in my bag!'

All the children laughed. They'd guessed it must be Rooney. Mrs Watkins screamed some more. She was on tiptoe on top of the chair, pointing at Rooney and crying for help. Then the bell went. All the children made for the door, and Nora made for the front of the class to pick up Rooney. But before anyone could leave the classroom, Mrs Starling, having heard the commotion, came striding into the room. She looked crosser than ever before. There was silence.

'Mrs Watkins, what is the matter?'

Mrs Watkins stammered that there was a rat in the classroom, but by this time Nora had scooped Rooney up and was stuffing him up her sleeve, out of sight.

'A rat?' said Mrs Starling. 'Here in the school?'

'Y... Y... Yes,' replied Mrs Watkins.

'Mmmmmmm,' said Mrs Starling, slowly. 'I can certainly smell a rat.'

Her eyes darted around the room. 'There doesn't seem to be a rat here now.'

'But there was... a minute ago... definitely,' said Mrs Watkins. 'I saw it. I'm rather frightened of mice and rats,' she added, rather meekly.

'So we can see,' said Mrs Starling. She prowled around the classroom as if she were a cat about to gobble up her prey. She looked at each of the children in turn.

'Does anyone know about what has happened here?' she demanded.

No one spoke.

'Gary,' she said, 'have you seen a rat in the classroom today?'

'No,' said Gary, sort of honestly. It was a hamster he had seen, not a rat, but he wasn't going to tell Mrs Starling. She stopped in front of Naughty Nora.

'Now then, Nora Grace. Have you seen a rat in the class today?'

'No,' said Nora, as truthfully as Gary Wild.

But all the while that Mrs Starling was talking, Rooney had been burrowing his way up Nora's sleeve, and at that very moment his head poked out from underneath Nora's jumper. Naughty Nora gulped.

'What,' said Mrs Starling, 'is that?'

'Oh,' said Naughty Nora, picking up Rooney. 'This? Oh, this is Rooney, my pet hamster.'

Nora turned to Mrs Watkins, who had now got down from her chair and was standing next to her. 'There's nothing to be frightened of, Mrs Watkins, he's a very friendly fellow.' She smiled and passed Rooney towards her teacher.

Mrs Watkins fainted. She took one look at Rooney, her legs crumpled and she fell to the floor.

'Oh lummy,' said Naughty Nora. 'I don't think she likes animals.'

Well, I hardly need to tell you what happened next. Naughty Nora got into yet more trouble. Mrs Starling gave her a severe talking-to. So did Mum and Dad when Mrs Starling phoned them up and told them what had happened. So did Mrs Watkins the next morning, and for several other mornings after that. And from that day on, Rooney had to stay at home when Naughty Nora went to school.

But that wasn't quite the end of the matter. A few weeks later, Sue, the priest who came into the school, had an idea for a special service at church. She wanted the whole school to come along. It was the feast day of St Francis of Assisi, and he was someone who really loved animals, just like Naughty Nora did.

The idea was to have a service where not just people came to church, but animals as well. Everyone could give thanks to God for the wonders of creation and especially for animals, and could pray that they might treat animals a bit better.

Everyone thought it was a brilliant idea, and everyone was encouraged to bring their pet to the animal service. But, as a final punishment for bringing Rooney into school, Nora was told that he couldn't come. 'He's caused enough trouble already,' said Mrs Watkins, 'and this might just help you learn to be a bit more sensible.'

Naughty Nora had never been keen on 'sensible'. 'Sensible' never seemed fun. 'You can bring another animal in,' she had been told, but Nat had already said that he was going to take Pickles. Mum said that she couldn't borrow the parrot from the end of the road, and Dad said it would serve her right if she didn't have any animal to take, because she'd been so naughty.

When the day of the animal service arrived, Nora was feeling very fed up. But, at the last minute, determined to take something to the service, she had another one of her bright ideas. She ran into the garden to collect some animals to take to church.

In church, everyone was gathered—mums and dads, grandmas and grandads, uncles and aunts, teachers and animals. Mrs Watkins, who didn't like hamsters or mice, had brought in her tortoise, which she had had since she was a little girl. Mrs Starling had brought her dog—a large Alsatian. Nat was sitting with Mum and Dad, and Pickles was curled up on his lap.

Junji had brought his gerbil. Amanda Goodchild was sitting with her mum and their very well-behaved poodle. Tabita had brought a rather fine-looking guinea pig. Keenan had brought his collection of stick insects, and Cameron had borrowed his grandad's Scottish terrier. Joseph, whose Dad worked at the local farm shop, had brought a donkey. She was tethered at the back next to the font.

Gary Wild was sitting in the front pew with a big grin on his face. On his lap was a large glass container, and in it was a snake. Everyone was nudging each other and pointing. So he did have a pet snake, after all! They were amazed. After the service, the whole class, including Mrs Watkins, had to say sorry to him, for no one had ever believed his story.

Sitting in the pew at the very back, having come in after everyone else, and ever so slightly late, was Naughty Nora. On her lap was a jam jar, and no one could see what was in it.

Sue welcomed everyone. They sang a hymn. There was a reading from the Bible about lions sitting down with lambs and about peace in all the world. Then Sue talked about how we share the world with animals and how we really ought to look after them a bit better. Then all the people and all the animals were invited to come to the front for a blessing.

That afternoon, Sue said prayers of thanks and blessing for dogs, cats, guinea pigs, hamsters, rabbits, Mrs Watkins' tortoise, Gary Wild's snake and Joe's donkey. Last of all, Nora came to the front. She wished she had Rooney with her and, in her head, she said a prayer thanking God for her hamster.

'Is it a prayer just for you?' said Sue when Nora knelt down.

'No, not just me. I've brought some animals with me.'

Nora reached inside the jam jar and brought out a handful of fat, pink, wiggly earthworms. She had dug them up in the garden before coming out.

'I've brought these along,' she said.

Sue looked at the worms writhing around in Nora's hand and she smiled.

'Thank you, God, for these beautiful worms—for the way they enrich the soil and help us get our crops. And thank you for Nora. Thank you for her love of life and all the fun and adventure she brings to her friends.'

They both said 'Amen'. Everyone giggled a bit when they saw Nora walking back to her place with a handful of worms, but Sue said how lovely it was that there were creatures great and small gathered in the church that day.

That night, Nora lay in bed with the curtains open and looked out of her window, up into the night sky. She had a warm feeling inside her. The world felt a friendly and wonderful place. She felt as if she wanted to reach out and hold the stars and embrace the world. She was part of this incredible universe that God had made. In fact, it all seemed so beautiful that it made her cry, and when her mum came into her bedroom to see what the matter was, she could only splutter, 'The worms. The stars. The world. It's all so lovely. I don't want it ever to end.'

Mum held her hand.

'It is a beautiful world,' she said. 'It was made by a beautiful God, and even when it does end, not one bit of it will be lost, for everything will be gathered together into the fantastic heaven that God has got ready for us.'

Naughty Nora gave her mum a big squeeze. She jumped up and stood at the window and looked out into the night. There were still tears in her eyes, but there was also a smile on her face. She stretched out her hands as wide as they could go. It felt as if she was holding the whole universe in her arms— and, in a way, she was, for God gives us the gift of life and the promise of a life that lasts for ever.

'Oh, thank you, God!' she shouted to the heavens.

Questions to explore with children

What is your favourite animal? Do you have a pet? What do you think your teacher would say if you brought your pet into school without asking first?

I wonder why Nora started crying at the end of the story? Have you ever felt as if the world is so lovely that it has made you want to cry?

Jesus says...

'Aren't two sparrows sold for only a penny? But your Father knows when any one of them falls to the ground.'
MATTHEW 10:29

God loves all the animals and the whole of creation. God loves us. In the Bible there are lots of stories about God caring for the whole world and asking us to care for it as well.

In the Bible there is a lovely passage about heaven—where all the animals live in peace with each other (Isaiah 11:5–7). This was the bit that Sue read out and talked about. There is also the wonderful story of Noah's ark, which also tells us about God's love for the world and all the creatures in it (Genesis 6:9—8:22).

Prayer

Big-hearted God,
we thank you for the beauty and wonder of your creation.
Help us to look after it with the same love that we see in Jesus,
and fill our hearts with love for you. Amen

Retelling the story

Bringing one or two animals along to help tell the story will obviously be useful but, if possible, do try to bring some worms so that you can dramatize the moment when Naughty Nora shows the worms to Sue. You could ask the children to guess what Nora has in the jam jar. Jumping up on a chair in imitation of Mrs Watkins will also add to the dramatic effect.

Bible index

Old Testament

New Testament

Enjoyed

this book?

Write a review—we'd love to hear what you think.
Email: reviews@brf.org.uk

Keep up to date—receive details of our new books as they happen.
Sign up for email news and select your interest groups at:
www.brfonline.org.uk/findoutmore/

Follow us on Twitter @brfonline

By post—to receive new title information by post (UK only), complete the form below and post to: BRF Mailing Lists, 15 The Chambers, Vineyard, Abingdon, Oxfordshire, OX14 3FE

Your Details		
Name		
Address		
Town/City		Post Code
Email		

Your Interest Groups (*Please tick as appropriate)		
☐ Advent/Lent	☐ Messy Church	
☐ Bible Reading & Study	☐ Pastoral	
☐ Children's Books	☐ Prayer & Spirituality	
☐ Discipleship	☐ Resources for Children's Church	
☐ Leadership	☐ Resources for Schools	

Support your local bookshop
Ask about their new title information schemes.

CPSIA information can be obtained at www.ICGtesting.com
Printed in the USA
BVOW04s1405070415

395095BV00027B/380/P